NAVIGATING TAX LAND

AUTHOR VOICE

NAVIGATING Tax Land

Simple Ways to Save Money on April 15th

DAVID R. PETERS

CPA, CFP®, CLU, CPCU

Navigating Tax Land: Simple Ways to Save Money on April 15th

Library of Congress Control Number: 2025927541
ISBN: 978-1-969935-37-4 (paperback) 9781969935381 (ebook)

Editors: Abigail Dengler, Jennifer Casey
Cover and Interior Design: Emma Elzinga

Printed in the United States of America

First Edition

3 West Garden Street, Ste. 718
Pensacola, FL 32502

Published by Author Voice Publishing
An Imprint of Indigo River Publishing
www.authorvoicepublishing.com

Ordering Information:

Quantity sales: Special discounts are available on quantity purchases by corporations, associations, and others. For details, contact the publisher at the address above.

Orders by US trade bookstores and wholesalers: Please contact the publisher at the address above.

The content presented in this book is for informational purposes only, is general in nature, and is not intended to and should not be relied upon or construed as financial, investment, or estate planning advice. This does not constitute an offer to sell or a solicitation to buy any security, investment, or planning product. Past performance is not indicative of future results. All investments involve risk, including the possible loss of principal. Please consult with a financial advisor to assess your individual situation.

Financial and investment advisory services offered through Peters Financial LLC. David Peters also offers tax services through Peters Tax Preparation & Consulting, PC, and insurance services through David Peters Insurance Agency LLC. Peters Tax Preparation & Consulting, PC, and David Peters Insurance Agency LLC are affiliated with Peters Financial LLC through common ownership. Clients or prospective clients are never obligated to use Peters Tax Preparation & Consulting, PC, or David Peters Insurance Agency LLC as part of any financial planning or investment management services offered by Peters Financial LLC.

Contents

Introduction: Results over Style Points 1

1. Saving Money on Itemized Deductions 5

2. "Time Traveling" with Last-Minute Tax Moves. 27

3. Side Gigs and Extra Income: What You Can Deduct 41

4. College Costs: Tax Tips for Sending a Kid to School 57

5. From Diapers to Deductions: Tax Breaks for Raising Kids 69

6. Airbnb and Rentals: What Hosts Can Deduct 83

7. How to Save a Few Bucks in Retirement. 101

8. Your Most Common Tax Questions, Answered 119

About the Author 133

INTRODUCTION

Results over Style Points

He stared at me blankly over his thick glasses. I could tell he was studying me and trying to figure out what I was going to do next. Admittedly, the long pause made me uncomfortable. After all, I had just given him a strategy that I knew was brilliant. I knew this because I had proposed the same strategy in graduate school for a project. I remember my professor praising me for my "keen sense of detail." Certainly, my boss in the real world was just so blown away by what I just told him that he was speechless . . . *Right?*

"Dave, there is no way he is going to do that," he said to me as he shook his head.

"But it could save him mon—" I didn't even get the full sentence out.

"Yes, but he will never do it." His coke-bottle glasses had slipped lower on his nose. "He is never going to be able to create a pension plan that is in line with the IRS requirements and get it funded without getting professional help from someone. He doesn't want to pay anyone. You have to give people stuff they can use and will actually do. You don't get paid for style points. You get paid to help them get the best tax result possible. Most people don't care how imaginative the strategy is. They only care if it is effective. Is it going to save them a few bucks on their return?"

I learned many hard lessons as a young CPA. I learned how to respond to IRS letters, how to help clients understand their tax returns, and even how to write up a tax research memorandum. However, all of those lessons pale in comparison to this one. We see many strategies for lowering your tax liability. We see news spots about how to "game the system," and we hear legends about "tax loopholes." Even at the conferences that I attend, practitioners are often deemed brilliant for the tax strategies they present. The more obscure and creative it is, the more brilliant it must be.

The problem? Come tax season, most everyone is overwhelmed. People are wondering whether their withholding was enough. They are scrounging through files and old papers, trying to find documentation of that one deduction they thought they made. They may even be bracing themselves for the inevitable fight that they have with their spouse each year. The point is that no one really feels good about tax time. It is a time that brings out the worst financial stress of the year.

This time of year always reminds me of when I was sixteen years old, and my dad took me to the local library on a day in late March. He pulled various forms from the rainbow-colored wire baskets. Above the stacks of papers, the sign read "IRS Forms." He handed me the forms and simply said, "Here. You are going to learn how to do this."

I spent the next few nights at the kitchen table trying to make sense of the instructions I read. More realistically, I spent those nights trying to look as much like an object of pity as possible. I kept hoping my dad would swoop in and just work through my taxes for me. He never did. He wanted me to understand even at a young age that making money necessarily involved filing taxes. It was something everyone had to do. While I don't get stressed out about my own return anymore, I still recognize that overwhelmed look in someone's eyes. The look that says, "Please rescue me from this maze of forms!" It is the same look that I had in my eyes at sixteen!

Those nights marked my first entry into what I often call "Tax Land." I call it Tax Land because stepping into the world of taxes feels much like stepping into a foreign territory. First, you are struck by a whole new language (*deductions, exemptions, withholdings, credits, and itemizations—words that sound familiar but mean something different here).* Then, you come to find the landscape is much broader and more varied than you thought it was (all these *different forms and strategies for different types of income).* You also come to learn that Tax Land has its own complex history, deeply intertwined with our own culture and current events (*from wartime tax expansions to debates over who should pay more and how tax policy reflects our social priorities).* As if all that wasn't overwhelming enough, everyone's tax situation is different—and it is difficult (if not impossible) to come up with a strategy that will help everyone.

In short, Tax Land is a strange place! And as my boss reminded me long ago, most clients don't care how brilliant the strategy is. They only care if the technique can save them a few bucks and is something they can do easily. They need a guide who can show them the possible routes and keep them from getting lost along the way.

In the pages that follow, I am not going to lay out brilliant and innovative tax strategies that take tens of hours and an accounting degree to implement. Rather, we are going to talk about the simplest and most approachable yet *effective* strategies that I have found in my over twenty-year career as a tax practitioner that are helpful to many tax clients. If you are not currently doing them, they might help you keep a few dollars in your pocket—rather than giving them to Uncle Sam on April 15.

Notice that I said "many" clients find these strategies helpful—not "all." Again, everyone's tax situation is different. You'll notice by scanning the table of contents that some chapters may be just what you need, while others don't apply to you right now. In some instances, you just may not be the target of that particular government tax break. However, if you don't know what the available tax breaks are, it is tough to take advantage of them. So focus on the chapters that apply best to you, and skim the others—you may find tips you can store away for the future. Above all, awareness is the key!

When we're able to understand our tax return, we not only decrease the confusion, anxiety, and overwhelm—we take more of our financial future into our own hands. If you are looking for a simple guide through Tax Land to take more control over your finances, this is the book for you.

CHAPTER 1

Saving Money on Itemized Deductions

"But I saved all my receipts!" Susan said with exasperated disbelief. "Don't more deductions mean I pay less taxes?"

"Well, yes—but only if your additional deductions are more than your standard deduction," I said calmly. However, I might as well have been talking in ancient Aramaic. Susan just stared at me blankly.

Susan had been my client for several years, and I could certainly understand her frustration. She was learning a hard lesson. Deductions are one of, if not the most, foundational ways to save on taxes. Many who have been through more than a few tax seasons understand that deductions are expenses that decrease your taxable income and, therefore, save you money on taxes. Yet even this foundational tool has plenty of its own quirks that even experienced taxpayers don't realize. The first of those is the standard deduction.

What in the world is a standard deduction? Many people don't realize that our tax code is written so that it's possible for someone to have more itemized deductions but not actually get any tax benefit. It may seem unfair, but it's actually because the government gives us each a "freebie," otherwise known as the standard deduction.

Each year, the government gives taxpayers two options. Option 1 is to add up all your itemized deductions and deduct that total from your gross income. Itemized deductions mainly consist of out-of-pocket medical expenses, taxes, mortgage interest, and charitable contributions. However, Option 2, which many aren't aware of, is that you can also choose to deduct the standard deduction: an amount that is the same for everyone regardless of income, employment, or any other status. The standard deduction amount increases a little bit each year due to inflation. You are entitled to take either the standard deduction amount for that year or your itemized deductions, but not both.

Of course, you normally want to take whichever one is higher—more deductions usually mean less taxes.[1] For example, let's say the standard deduction is $15,750, and you have $5,000 in mortgage interest and $6,000 in deductible charitable contributions.[2] You should take the standard deduction, since your itemized deductions only add up to $11,000 ($6,000 + $5,000 = $11,000).

But what if you have $2,000 of additional charitable contribution receipts you forgot about? Would that make a difference? If you add the additional $2,000 to the $11,000 of itemized deductions you already have, that's $13,000 of deductions—still not more than the $15,750 standard deduction in our example. So those additional charitable receipts do not make a difference, and you're still better off taking the standard deduction. Incidentally, this is what was happening to my

---

1 It is possible to have a situation in which you would take the lower of your itemized deductions or your standard deduction. You might do this if it allowed you to save more money on your state income tax return. In other words, your federal tax bill was a little higher (because you took a lower deduction amount), but you saved a significant amount more on your state income taxes. This will be the rarest of rare cases, though!

2 Starting in 2026, there is a 0.5 percent AGI floor on itemized charitable contributions. This means that you must contribute over 0.5 percent of your adjusted gross income to get any tax benefit for your charitable contributions. Also, non-itemizing taxpayers can take a limited deduction for charitable contributions even if they don't itemize (starting in 2026). In this example, we are talking specifically about itemized charitable contributions.

client, Susan. She had more itemized deductions, just not enough to exceed her standard deduction.

Until you reach a point at which you have more itemized deductions than the standard deduction, additional tax deductions won't help. Your tax bill won't be any lower.

However, once your itemized deductions *exceed* your standard deduction, there are many opportunities to save money with more itemized deductions. In this chapter, you'll learn ways you may be able to save money on itemized deductions—and which opportunities are a waste of time.

Do I Need to Add Up All My Medical Receipts?

One of the most common and substantial itemized deductions is medical expenses. The cost of medical expenses in the United States is astronomical. According to the American Medical Association, US health care spending topped a whopping $4.3 trillion in 2021—a 2.7 percent increase compared to the prior year. In 2020, the increase was more than 10 percent from 2019![3] Americans continue to spend more and more each year on prescriptions, doctors, and everyday health care items like eyeglasses and headache medicine. The obvious question is: Can you get *any* tax benefit from these items?

The good news is that most medical expenses are technically deductible, which means they *could* help you shave a few dollars off your tax bill. IRS Publication 502 lists several deductible medical expenses:

- Legal abortion costs
- Acupuncture

3 "Trends in Health Care Spending." *American Medical Association.* Last modified April 17, 2025. https://www.ama-assn.org/about/research/trends-health-care-spending.

- Alcohol or drug addiction treatment (including transportation costs to a support group like Alcoholics Anonymous)
- Costs paid for ambulance services
- Annual physical exams
- Costs paid for an artificial limb or teeth
- Bandages and medical supplies
- Birth control pills (if prescribed by a doctor)
- Body scan costs
- Breast pumps & supplies
- Breast reconstruction surgery
- Certain capital expenditures to accommodate a medical need (for example, adding an exit ramp to your home)
- Special design costs for your car (such as adding a hand brake)
- Chiropractor costs
- Christian Science Practitioner costs
- Contact lenses
- Crutches
- Dental treatment
- Diagnostic devices (like a blood sugar test kit for a diabetic)
- Disabled dependent care expenses
- Eye examination and surgery costs (including Lasik)
- Eyeglasses
- Fertility enhancement costs (like in vitro fertilization)
- Guide dog or service animal costs (like training, food, grooming, and veterinary care)
- Health insurance premiums (including Medicare premiums)

- Hearing aids
- Hospital services
- Costs for a special home for those who are intellectually or developmentally disabled
- Lab fees
- Lead-based paint removal costs
- Legal fees necessary to authorize treatment for mental illness
- Lodging costs necessary for medical care
- Long-term care insurance premiums (up to a certain amount specified by the IRS each year)
- Meals at a hospital or similar institution if the principal reason for being there is to receive medical care
- Medicine and insulin costs
- Nursing home costs
- Nursing services (like helping with bathing, toileting, and giving medication)
- Necessary surgeries (not cosmetic in nature)
- Osteopath costs
- Oxygen and oxygen equipment costs
- Pregnancy test kits
- Psychiatric, psychologist, and psychoanalysis costs
- Special education costs (prescribed by a doctor)
- Legal sterilization procedure costs
- Stop-smoking programs
- Special telephone equipment for those who are deaf, hard of hearing, or have a speech disability

- Additional costs for a television to be adapted for those who are deaf (which displays subtitles)
- Therapy costs (if they are a part of medical treatment)
- Transplant costs of organs
- Transportation costs to or from a facility to receive medical care
- Vasectomy costs
- Weight-loss programs
- Wheelchairs
- Wigs for a person who has lost their hair due to disease
- X-rays

Most people who see this list are normally surprised by everything covered—there's a good chance that at least a couple of these apply to you now, and it's nearly certain more will apply to you in the future. However, before you start counting all the taxes you'll save, remember three things:[4]

1. Only payments NOT reimbursed by insurance or a Health Savings Account (HSA) are deductible (we'll talk more about HSAs later).
2. The expense must generally be paid for you, your spouse, or a dependent.
3. You will only see a tax benefit if your medical expense deductions exceed a certain percentage of your income.

Let's start with the first two items. Essentially, they mean that only out-of-pocket costs are deductible. While the list above is massive and nearly any medical expense counts, the only deductible medical expenses are those you pay from your own wallet for you, your spouse, or your dependents. For example, say you receive a $1,000 bill from your

4 Sec. 213(a)

doctor. You receive an insurance reimbursement for $700, but the rest of it you pay for yourself. In that case, only $300 would be deductible ($1,000 - $700 = $300) on Schedule A of your tax return.

What if you pay $1,000 in medical expenses and none of it is reimbursed by insurance, but you reimburse yourself using $700 from your HSA? Again, in this instance, only $300 would be deductible on your tax return. The tax code says only medical expenses that are "not compensated for by insurance or otherwise" are deductible. In other words, you must spend your own money to receive the benefit of a tax deduction.

Will that $300 help me save money on my tax bill? The unfortunate answer is: "It depends." The Internal Revenue Code says a deduction is only available "to the extent that such (medical) expenses exceed 7.5 percent of adjusted gross income." For most people, AGI is all their income added together—wages, self-employment income, interest you earn from a bank account, and so on.[5] In other words, your out-of-pocket medical costs must exceed 7.5 percent of AGI before you see any tax benefit.

Say you have a job with $49,000 in wages. You also have $1,000 of interest income from an online savings account. You don't have any other sources of income. In this instance, your AGI is $50,000 ($49,000 + $1,000). 7.5 percent of your AGI would be $3,750 ($50,000 x 7.5%). If you only have $3,000 in out-of-pocket medical expenses, you cannot take a deduction; your out-of-pocket medical costs are not above $3,750. Your deduction for medical expenses will be zero.

What if you have $3,751 in medical expenses not reimbursed by insurance? In that case, your deduction is only for any amount above 7.5 percent of AGI. In other words, your deduction would only be $1 ($3,751 - $3,750)!

---

5 AGI technically also includes "above-the-line deductions" as well. Some common above-the-line deductions include deductible contributions to a health savings account, deductible contributions to an IRA, and deductible student loan interest. Above-the-line deductions are shown on Schedule 1.

The bottom line: Unless you have a lot of out-of-pocket medical expenses, it's very difficult to take a deduction. For many working people, it's often only when something medically catastrophic happens (such as a major surgery or cancer) that they can take a tax deduction. The government doesn't want to take on the role of being an insurance company, helping reimburse people for the medical costs they pay. Therefore, tax policies are formed so the government will only subsidize catastrophic medical costs that are beyond the means of most people (that is, 7.5 percent of their income).

Tips for Maximizing Savings: Medical Deductions

1. For most people, their AGI is usually just their salary (and possibly some interest, dividends, and capital gains). Take 7.5 percent of your income. Unless you have out-of-pocket medical costs that are larger than this number, there is no point in sending your medical receipts to your tax preparer. Most tax practitioners charge based on the time they spend working on your return, so don't send them information they don't need! This will help keep your preparation fees to a minimum.
2. Don't forget about medical mileage. The miles you drive primarily for medical reasons (for example, to see a specialist) are deductible. You should keep a log showing the date of your trip, the purpose of your trip (e.g., "See Dr. X about back pain"), and how many miles you drove. This will help if the IRS ever questions the deduction.
3. If your medical-related trips involve overnight travel, be sure to keep track of meals and hotel stays as well. Many people are surprised at how much money is involved in simply traveling

to see a doctor or specialist. Remember though—the overnight stay must be necessary to go see the doctor. If you are simply staying overnight at a hotel a few miles from your house, that is not deductible! You need to be far enough away from your home to necessitate an overnight stay.

4. If you know you will need medication or medical supplies soon after January 1, consider purchasing them before year-end so you can take the deduction sooner. For example, let's say it is December 27 of Year 1. You know you'll need medication during the first week in January of Year 2. If you purchase your medication now, it will be deductible on your Year 1 tax return. If you wait until January of Year 2, it will not be deductible until your Year 2 tax return. By purchasing now, you will push those deductions into the current year, allowing you to utilize them sooner!

What Taxes Are Deductible?

If you now know that you won't be able to take medical deductions this year, there are plenty of other deduction possibilities we'll cover. In fact, many clients are surprised to learn that certain taxes they routinely pay can help save money on their income tax bill. Real estate taxes, state income taxes, and personal property taxes (like the ones many people pay on their cars) are deductible on your federal income tax return. However, like most things in Tax Land, there are parameters.

You can only deduct $40,000 in taxes on your federal return.

Most people can only deduct up to $40,000 in taxes on their federal income tax returns in 2025.[6] While this sounds like a lot, it may not be nearly as much as you think. It's not unusual for my clients in high-cost-of-living areas (like San Francisco or Manhattan) to pay $20,000 or more in real estate taxes alone for a moderately priced home. That's about half of the full deduction amount right there!

You can't take a deduction for taxes you don't pay!

Like most things on your federal income tax return, the only deductible taxes are the ones you actually pay. As of this writing, Alaska, Florida, Nevada, South Dakota, Tennessee, Texas, Washington, and Wyoming do not have a state income tax. If you happen to live and work in one of those states, you will not have any state income taxes to deduct on your federal tax return.[7]

This concept is particularly important regarding real estate and personal property taxes. In many areas, these taxes are assessed at the end of the year. For instance, I typically receive my real estate tax bill for my property in Richmond, VA, in mid-December—but they are not due until mid-January. When I actually pay (December or January) could make a difference on my income tax return.

Let's say I receive my $3,000 real estate tax bill on December 15 in Year 1. It is not due until January 15 of Year 2. If I choose to pay it in December of Year 1, it will be deductible on my Year 1 income tax return. If I choose to pay it in January of Year 2, it will be deducted on

---

6 If you file a Married Filing Separately tax return, you can only deduct up to $20,000 in total taxes in 2025. Also, if you happen to be a partner in a partnership or an S corporation shareholder, you may be able to deduct more than $40,000 by making something called a PTE election. Check with your tax advisor if this applies to you or send me an email (david-petersprofessionaleducation.com)!

7 It is possible for a resident in a state without an income tax to pay state income taxes. Let's say that you have someone who lives in Florida but works in Georgia. They would probably have to file a nonresident tax return in Georgia and pay taxes there. They just wouldn't have to pay taxes in their resident state of Florida!

my Year 2 tax return. In other words, if I wait until the new year to pay, it will be a long time before I see the benefit of that deduction!

Don't forget: The most that anyone can deduct is $40,000 in 2025. Therefore, the only time it would benefit me to pay my real estate tax bill early is if I haven't already paid $40,000 in real estate taxes for that year. Let's go back to my example above. If I have already paid $40,000 in state income taxes in Year 1, then paying my real estate tax bill in Year 1 will not help me on my federal tax return. I have already hit my deduction limit on my federal tax return.

Note that there is no limit to the number of homes you can deduct real estate taxes on. For example, if I own three homes—one is my primary residence and two are vacation homes—I can only deduct mortgage interest on two homes (more on this later). However, I can deduct real estate taxes on any number of homes. The real estate taxes I pay on all three homes will generally be deductible as long as I don't go over that $40,000 limit!

If you bought a boat, the sales tax you paid could help!

The IRS allows you to take a deduction for the sales tax you pay instead of your state income taxes. You cannot deduct both—it must be one or the other. This could be helpful in two situations:

1. You live in a state without state income tax (see above), so deducting state income taxes is not an option (because you didn't pay any); or
2. You made a large purchase in which you paid a lot of sales tax, like a boat, a luxury car, or a motor home.

If you think your sales tax might be higher than your income tax, hold on to your receipts for that purchase. That way, if the IRS ever questions you about the deduction, you will have documentation showing you paid it.

Also, you can elect to deduct income taxes one year and then sales taxes the next. Normally, the best option is to choose whichever one is higher for a particular year, so you can get the highest deduction possible.

If you own a business, you may be able to deduct more.

If you are a partner in a partnership or an S corporation shareholder, you normally take all the income and deductions from your business on your own personal income tax return. We call these entities "pass-through" or "flow-through" entities because the income and deductions from the company "flow through" to you, the business owner. When this happens, you pick up the tab for the taxes your company generates.

Let's say you and your buddy are each 50 percent partners in a partnership. You divide everything equally, from your profits to the cost of printer toner. If your company made $100,000, the company would not typically pay any taxes on that amount. Instead, you would show $50,000 on your tax return (50 percent of the profits). Naturally, this would increase your tax bill because you are showing an additional $50,000 in income on both your federal and state income tax returns. Let's say your state charges a 12 percent income tax. That means you pay $6,000 in state income taxes on your share of the income ($50,000 x 12% = $6,000).

Would this additional $6,000 in state income taxes be deductible on your federal income tax return? Yes—as long as you haven't already hit the $40,000 deduction limit. Remember, the most anyone can deduct is $40,000. No matter what, you can't deduct more than that for state income taxes, real estate taxes, and personal property taxes on your personal income tax return.

What if you are already at that $40,000 limit? For example, what if you have already paid $40,000 in real estate taxes? If that's the case, you will normally not be able to take any deduction on your federal income tax return because you've already maxed out. That's not a great result: You paid $6,000 in state income taxes because of your business, but your tax deduction is zero on your federal return!

One way to get around this bad tax result is to do something called a pass-through entity (PTE) election. While every state is a little bit different, many offer you the ability to have your business pay its own state income taxes. The entity takes the deduction for the payment—and you have less income on your personal return to pay taxes on!

To illustrate this, let's go back to our example. If you let your partnership pay the state income taxes, only $44,000 of income flows through to you—$50,000 in partnership income minus the $6,000 in paid state income taxes. In other words, by letting the partnership pay the taxes, you now have $6,000 less in income to show on your personal return.

But what about that $40,000 limit on state income taxes? Well, it won't matter here because the deduction for the $6,000 is taken by the partnership, not you. The partnership can deduct as much in state income taxes as it wants. Only *you* have the $40,000 limit. By letting the partnership pay, you show less income on your personal return. Practically speaking, it's almost as if you are taking a higher deduction than what is allowed by the $40,000 limit, even though you are within the legal parameters.

While this can be a helpful election for a business owner, it's important to remember the rules around PTE elections vary by state, and planning can get very complex.[8] Also, remember—this is only possible in states that actually *have* an income tax. Before committing to make a PTE election, talk to a professional to make sure you know the details. In the right circumstances, this can save a small business owner significant tax money.

---

8 For example, it is possible to make a PTE election in one state but not another. It's also possible that states may treat the PTE election in different ways on the state tax return. One state may treat it as a tax credit, while another may treat it as excluded income. This can change the results, so just be sure to talk to a professional before doing this. This is not light stuff!

Tips for Maximizing Savings: Tax Deductions

1. If you haven't hit the $40,000 limit on federal tax deductions, make a *state* estimated tax payment or make a payment on your real estate tax bill by December 31. This allows you to take the full $40,000 deduction on your federal income tax return this year (rather than having to wait until next year).
2. If you own a business (S corporation or partnership), consider making a PTE election and having the company pay its own state income taxes. By doing this, you could potentially deduct more than the $40,000 limit at the federal level.
3. Keep track of your sales tax on big purchases like cars and boats. To take a deduction, you generally need to have documentation. While many people dislike the clutter created by receipts, it's important to remember that those receipts can lead to bigger deductions! Save a digital copy if you prefer, and always keep them until you know you don't need them!

Why Should I Pay Off My Mortgage? It Is My Biggest Deduction!

For most people, their mortgage is the largest and most significant loan they'll ever have. It also generates their biggest tax deduction. Mortgage interest is deductible on the first two homes a person owns. Obviously, the bigger the balance on the mortgage, the more interest you pay. The more interest you pay, the bigger your tax deduction.[9] Simple, right?

But here's the real deal. It is never worth it to keep a mortgage only for the tax deduction. Say you pay $5,000 in mortgage interest in a year, and you are in the 22 percent federal tax bracket. If that's the case, you will not save $5,000 on your tax bill. You'll only save about $1,100 ($5,000 x 22% tax bracket = $1,100 in tax savings). Why? Because there is a difference between credits and deductions. A tax credit reduces your tax bill dollar for dollar. A $5,000 *credit* will reduce your tax bill by $5,000. However, a *deduction* only reduces the income you pay taxes on. Mortgage interest is a tax deduction—not a credit.

That's a pretty bad deal if you think about it. You are paying $5,000 to the bank in interest on your loan, but you're only receiving $1,100 back in the form of a reduced tax bill. In other words, you are only getting 22 cents in benefits for every dollar you spend. That's not great—and certainly not a reason to keep yourself in thousands of dollars of debt!

Does that mean paying off a mortgage is *always* the best move? Well, maybe not. Let's say I have $100,000 in cash. I can pay off my mortgage, or I can invest this money in the market. If I know the interest rate on my mortgage is 4.5 percent, but I could earn 6 percent by investing my money in the markets, then it's mathematically better to just invest the money. I would make $6,000 on my investment ($100,000 x 6% = $6,000) and pay $4,500 less in mortgage interest ($100,000 x 4.5% = $4,500). I would make enough in the markets to cover my mortgage interest payment and have $1,500 to spare ($6,000 - $4,500 = $1,500)!

However, it's hard to know what your investments are actually going to do—and any form of investing involves risk. There's always a

9 Mortgage interest is only deductible on the first $750,000 of the mortgage principal (referred to as "acquisition indebtedness" in the Internal Revenue Code). In other words, if your mortgage balance is over $750,000, you won't be able to deduct all of your mortgage interest—just a portion of it (Sec. 163(h)(3)(F)).

chance I might make something less than 6 percent on those investments or even *lose* money. On the other hand, if I make the decision to pay off my mortgage, I no longer have access to that money. Once you pay something, the money is no longer in your account—and is not available for any other purpose. Simply put, you can't say it's *always* better to pay off a mortgage or *always* better to invest. It just depends on which option you are more comfortable with—paying down a debt and losing access to that money or investing it and knowing that markets could go down.

One thing is for sure, though: It's never worth it to keep a mortgage only for the tax deduction.

Tips for Maximizing Savings: Mortgage Interest

1. Mortgage interest is deductible on the first two personal residences. If you happen to have three personal residences, don't have a mortgage on all of them. It's better to keep a larger mortgage on your main home (personal residence) rather than have three smaller mortgages.
2. Mortgage interest on a rental property is deductible without any limit to the number of rental properties. Therefore, you could have three rental properties with a mortgage on each of them, and the mortgage interest on each loan is deductible. The two-residence limitation applies to personal residences, not rentals.
3. It's never worth it to just keep a mortgage for the tax deduction. There may be other reasons to keep a mortgage, but not for the tax benefits alone.

Should I Give to Charity This Year to Knock Down My Tax Bill?

My grandmother used to tell me not to "let the tail wag the dog" whenever she felt I was letting a small factor drive a much larger decision. It was her way of letting me know I was looking at a decision backward. I often find myself using the same words when dealing with clients asking about charitable contributions. They ask if they should give to charity to generate additional tax deductions. It is usually at this point that I blow their minds: It is *never* worth it to give to charity just for the tax deduction!

Before anyone starts sending hate tweets about me being a cold-hearted CPA, I want to point out that I did not say "giving to charity is a waste of money" or "you should never give to charity." I give to plenty of charities on a regular basis to support educational and community causes. I also occasionally give money to friends and family who are trying to do something positive. I truly do think charitable giving can make you a better person and help improve the world around you. My issue is not with charities or charitable giving. My issue is with someone's reason for giving: the tax deduction. It is backward thinking. It is letting the tail wag the dog.

Very similar to the mortgage interest example above, giving to charity is not a tax credit. It is a tax deduction, meaning that it is not a one-for-one tax benefit. If you are in the 22 percent federal tax bracket and you give $100 to charity, you only get $22 off your tax bill—not $100 ($100 x 22% = $22). You are spending $100 to get $22 back.[10] That's a bad deal. Therefore, giving to charity only for the tax deduction is silly. It makes no sense.

Let's reframe the question. If you are already planning to give to charity, are there any strategies available to maximize your deductions?

---

10 Starting in 2026, there is a 0.5 percent AGI floor on charitable contributions. Therefore, this example assumes you are already above the 0.5 percent floor.

Now *that's* a great question. Yes! Without a doubt, there are!

Charitable contributions are probably the itemized deduction you have the most control over. You can't really control when you are going to get sick or see a doctor, so medical deductions are out of your control. You would never want to pay more taxes or interest on your mortgage. Charitable contributions are the one place a client can easily control the amount of their deduction. This makes it a great area for planning—but only if you are charitably inclined!

Bunching Up Deductions

Remember what I said at the beginning of this chapter: Everyone gets the higher of their itemized deductions or their standard deduction. Let's say the standard deduction is $13,000, and your only itemized deductions are mortgage interest of $5,000 and real estate taxes of $2,000.[11] If that's the case, you would have to give more than $6,000 in deductible contributions to charity before you would see any tax benefit ($13,000 - $5,000 - $2,000 = $6,000). If you don't give at least that much, your standard deduction will still be higher than your itemized deductions, so you wouldn't get a tax benefit.

One strategy you can use is simply to double up on contributions. Let's return to our example above. Instead of giving $5,000 each year to charity, you give $10,000 one year and then nothing the next. You then repeat the process for as long as you wish to support the charity. In the years you give $10,000, you will have enough to itemize your deductions:

$5,000 Mortgage interest

+ $2,000 real estate taxes

+ $10,000 deductible charitable contributions[12]

Total itemized deductions: $17,000

---

11 Remember, the standard deduction amount is normally adjusted for inflation each year. Here we are just using $13,000 for the purposes of our example!

12 Again, ignoring the 0.5 percent AGI floor in this example.

Either way, you'd be giving $10,000 over two years. But if you separated them out and took the standard deduction each year, you'd have a total of $26,000 in deductions (the standard deduction x 2), whereas if you doubled up, you'd have a total of $30,000 in deductions ($17,000 one year and the standard $13,000 the next). That's $4,000 more in deductions over two years without spending any more out of pocket!

This simple planning move can help you cut a few dollars off your tax bill. But what about the charity? Doesn't it hurt their budgeting for you to double up on your contributions one year and give nothing the next? Well, it would—if it weren't for the donor-advised fund (DAF).

What is a DAF? Sounds like a musical group from the '80s I missed!

Once, I actually had a client utter the words above. He was convinced I made up the acronym DAF! But in the world of finance, DAF means "donor-advised fund"—it's basically a vehicle that allows you to make charitable contributions in a tax-advantageous way without hurting charities' budgets.

When you open a DAF, you can normally fund it whenever you like. The money inside the fund grows tax-free until you choose what charity to support. Let's return to our example above. You could put $10,000 into a DAF in Year 1. You would also get a tax deduction in Year 1 for $10,000. However, you could choose to have the donor-advised fund transfer $5,000 to your favorite charity in Year 1 and then the remaining $5,000 in Year 2. There will be no hardship on their budget, and you can execute on your tax strategy of doubling up on charitable contributions in Year 1 and giving nothing in Year 2.

DAFs are widely available. You can open one through nearly any investment brokerage or financial advising firm. However, once you contribute money to a DAF, you can't get it back. You must use the funds for charitable purposes. Also, you should talk to a financial advisor or professional about how to invest the money and what fees are associated with the accounts.[13] But if used correctly, a DAF can be a great way to get the most out of your charitable giving.

What about donating property, like a car or bitcoin?

As a general rule, you typically pay taxes on any gains you have on the sale or disposal of property. For example, if I sell stock, I generally have to pay taxes on the gains (the difference between how much I sold it for and how much I bought it for). One important exception, though, is giving property to charity. If you give the property away to charity, you can take a deduction—and you don't have to pay taxes on the gains. A win-win!

By IRS standards, the definition of "property" here is quite broad. It basically covers anything of value that isn't cash: not just buildings and land but also vehicles, furniture, and artwork, as well as stocks, bonds, and other forms of intangible property. It should be noted that charitable donations of virtual currency, like Bitcoin, are considered to be contributions of property for tax purposes. So, when given to charity, the rules we covered above generally apply to each of these as well.

Of course, always check with a charity first to see if they are willing to accept a gift of property. If they want cash, you must sell your vehicle first and then give them the cash. This may still be okay, but you would be taxed on the capital gains from the sale of the car. You would need to make sure the tax benefits from making the charitable contribution of cash outweigh the taxes generated from the capital gains.

If they do accept property, the calculation of the deduction can get a little complicated. However, in general, many contributions of property will result in a deduction equal to the fair market value of the property contributed. There are certain limitations on how much

---

13 Remember—all investments have risk. It is possible to gain and lose money in the markets. Yes, I truly am a financial advisor!

may be contributed to charity each year, but this normally only affects people who are retired or just have a low-income year.[14]

The Bottom Line

Remember that medical expenses, mortgage interest, taxes, and charitable contributions are itemized deductions. The only way you can receive tax benefits from these items is if your total itemized deductions are greater than the standard deduction. If the standard deduction is more, none of these strategies will help! However, by knowing the options available to you, there are plenty of strategies to explore for meaningful savings.

Tips for Maximizing Savings: Charitable Contributions

1. You should never give to charity only for the tax deduction. However, if you are passionate about giving something, why not give in the most tax-advantageous way possible? You can generally only take a charitable contribution deduction in a year in which you itemize.
2. To surpass the standard deduction, you can double up your charitable donations one year, then take the standard deduction the next. If you put the money into a DAF, you'll give the same amount out of pocket but get more deductions *and* can dispense the funds in line with the charity's budgeting needs.

---

14 In 2025, you cannot give more than 60 percent of your AGI in cash charitable contributions to public charities. You can also only give 30 percent in property contributions to public charities.

3. On large gifts in low-income years, it is possible your entire deduction may not be allowed. There are limitations to how much you can give to charity: typically, up to **60 percent of your adjusted gross income (AGI)** for **cash donations** to public charities, and **30 percent of your AGI** for **property donations**. Starting in **2026**, there will also be a **0.5 percent AGI minimum** (or "floor") before charitable deductions can be taken. If you are thinking about giving a large gift to charity right after you retire, make sure you aren't running up against limitations!

CHAPTER 2

"Time Traveling" with Last-Minute Tax Moves

"Can't you do anything about this?" my client, Tom, asked after we finished reviewing his tax return. As my grandmother would say, he was not a happy camper. Tom was a construction contractor with a good reputation locally for his quality work. However, he had a family of four, and the associated costs made things financially tight. I just had the unfortunate task of telling him he owed money on his taxes this year. "Isn't there anything we can do?" I could see the desperation in his face and his voice.

Whenever you put together a tax return, you are nearly always preparing it for the year that has already happened. We prepare last year's tax return in April of this year. Since a tax return is essentially a summary of everything that happened in the prior year, the moves on the board are very limited once the calendar flips to January. For the most part, unless I happened to do something in the prior year that would result in a tax deduction or credit—like those covered in the previous chapter—I am usually out of luck. I can do things now to affect the tax return that I will prepare next April—but that doesn't help clients like Tom who are looking for anything to help reduce that bill in the moment!

Notice what I said: The moves on the board are limited, but not gone! The good news is that there are certain types of behavior the government believes in incentivizing so much that they will give you a deduction under the right circumstances, even after the tax year is over. These behaviors include saving for retirement and saving for future health care costs.

Make an Individual Retirement Account (IRA) Contribution

An IRA is a type of retirement account not associated with your employer. They are widely available. You can open one online, at a bank, or with a financial advisor. You can make contributions to an IRA if you have compensation (like wages from a job or compensation from self-employment). You can generally contribute up to a certain limit each year ($7,000 in 2025). If you are fifty or older, you can contribute more ($8,000 in 2025). There are two basic types of IRAs: Roth and traditional.

Roth IRA

The first type of retirement account is a Roth IRA. And while we're talking about how to save on your taxes, contributions to a Roth IRA are actually never deductible. So why are we talking about it here if it doesn't lower your taxes *now*? Because the Roth option saves you money on taxes in the future.

With a Roth IRA, when you retire, you can pull any money built up in the Roth IRA tax-free. You can't take a deduction on the money you contribute up front, but the money in the Roth will grow tax-free (if markets cooperate), and then it can be distributed tax-free.

In fact, if you make too much money, you can't contribute to a Roth anymore. Take a look. Here are the phaseout limits for 2025:

<table>
<tr><th>If your filing status is:</th><th>And your Modified AGI is:</th><th>Then you can contribute:</th></tr>
<tr><td rowspan="3">Married Filing Jointly (MFJ) or Qualifying Widow(er)</td><td>Less than $236,000</td><td>Up to the limit</td></tr>
<tr><td>Equal to or greater than $236,000 but less than $246,000</td><td>A reduced amount</td></tr>
<tr><td>Equal to or greater than $246,000</td><td>Zero</td></tr>
</table>

<table>
<tr><th>If your filing status is:</th><th>And your Modified AGI is:</th><th>Then you can contribute:</th></tr>
<tr><td rowspan="2">Married Filing Separately (MFS) and you lived with your spouse at any time during the tax year</td><td>Less than $10,000</td><td>A reduced amount</td></tr>
<tr><td>Equal to or greater than $10,000</td><td>Zero</td></tr>
</table>

If your filing status is:	And your Modified AGI is:	Then you can contribute:
Single, Head of Household, or Married Filing Separately and you did not live with your spouse at any time during the tax year	Less than $150,000	Up to the limit
	Equal to or greater than $150,000 but less than $165,000	A reduced amount
	Equal to or greater than $165,000	Zero

As the tables above show, the phaseout limit varies based on your filing status. If you are married filing jointly, your income can be higher than if you were single.

Evaluate your income levels and see if you qualify to contribute to a Roth. If so, and you don't need to reduce your taxes immediately, save yourself on taxes in the future. But if you need a tax reduction immediately, a traditional IRA is your best bet.

Traditional IRA

In contrast to a Roth, contributions to a traditional IRA may be deductible. Usually, anyone can contribute to a traditional IRA if they have income from wages or self-employment (compensation). That said, whether you are able to take a tax deduction for your contribution generally depends on if you have a retirement plan at work and your income level.

If you don't have a retirement plan at work, you can contribute up to the IRS limit for the year ($7,000 in 2025 or $8,000 in 2025, if you are fifty or older). Every dollar you contribute will be deductible.[15] If you have access to a retirement plan at work (like a 401(k) or 403(b)), it gets a little more complicated. In that circumstance, your ability to take a deduction may be limited if you or your spouse makes too much money. Here are the tables applicable to that circumstance for 2025:

If your filing status is:	**And your Modified AGI is:**	**Then you can take:**
Married Filing Jointly (MFJ) with a spouse that is covered by a plan at work (but you are NOT covered by a plan at work)	$236,000 or less	Full deduction up to the limit
	More than $236,000, but less than $246,000	A partial deduction
	$246,000 or more	No deduction

15 The amount you can contribute is limited to the lesser of your compensation for the year or the IRS limit, whichever is less.

If your filing status is:	And your Modified AGI is:	Then you can take:
Married Filing Separately (MFS) with a spouse that is covered by a plan at work (but you are NOT covered by a plan at work)	Less than $10,000	A partial deduction
	$10,000 or more	No deduction

If your filing status is:	And your Modified AGI is:	Then you can take:
Single, Head of Household, or Married Filing Separately and you did not live with your spouse at any time during the tax year (and you ARE covered by a plan at work)	$79,000 or less	Full deduction up to the limit
	More than $79,000 but less than $89,000	A partial deduction
	$89,000 or more	No deduction

If your filing status is:	And your Modified AGI is:	Then you can take:
Married Filing Jointly (MFJ) or Qualifying Widow(er) (and you ARE covered by a plan at work)	$126,000 or less	Full deduction up to the limit
	More than $126,000 but less than $146,000	A partial deduction
	$146,000 or more	No deduction

If your filing status is:	And your Modified AGI is:	Then you can take:
Married Filing Separately (MFS) and you lived with your spouse at any time during the tax year (and you ARE covered by a plan at work)	Less than $10,000	A partial deduction
	$10,000 or more	No deduction

To be clear, you can always contribute the full amount (up to the IRS limit) each year to a traditional IRA as long as you have compensation.

However, if you are covered by a retirement plan at work, not all your contributions will be deductible.

While the tax deduction is nice on the front end when you make the IRA contribution, the results when the money is distributed in retirement are not as good. Like a Roth IRA, funds contributed to a traditional IRA grow tax-free inside the account. However, when the funds are distributed in retirement, they are taxable income to the recipient. This could amount to a lot of taxable income in retirement if the markets did well since the IRA was opened. For this reason, it can be helpful to have a mix of Roth and traditional IRA contributions.

How does this help you after the tax year is over? You can contribute to a traditional IRA up until April 15 and take a deduction for your contribution.[16] Those deductions will count toward the previous tax year, as long as you designate them that way. For example, if you want the contribution to count for 2025, you simply need to indicate that on your check or on your electronic contribution (if you are making the contribution through a website).

This rule within the Internal Revenue Code gives you lots of flexibility. You can literally put together your entire tax return, figure out how much you owe, and then contribute to a traditional IRA to reduce your owed taxes. It's almost like going back in time! However, income limitations mean that not everyone can take advantage of this deduction.

Make a Health Savings Account (HSA) Contribution

Another action the government incentivizes is contributing to a Health

16 You can contribute to both a traditional and a Roth IRA at the same time, but total contributions cannot exceed the IRS limit for the year. For example, in 2025, you could contribute $3,500 to a traditional IRA and $3,500 to a Roth IRA. However, you could not contribute $7,000 to each of them.

Savings Account (HSA)—so much so that you can "time-travel" and reduce your taxable income with an HSA contribution.

An HSA is exactly what it sounds like. It is a way to save some money on taxes while saving up to pay for medical expenses. You can take a tax deduction for any money you contribute to an HSA. There are no issues with income limits. And just like the traditional IRA, you can make contributions all the way up until April 15—and count the deduction for the prior year.

There is one limitation. You *must* work for an employer that offers a high-deductible health plan (HDHP). These days, many employers do. The IRS dictates what constitutes an HDHP, based on a minimum deductible and maximum out-of-pocket costs. Most employers will indicate in their open enrollment packets each year which plans are considered HDHP, so they are easy to identify. If you are self-employed and buy your health insurance through the marketplace, you can also purchase an HDHP. Either way, you can only contribute to an HSA if you have an HDHP.

Some employers will make contributions on an employee's behalf to their HSA. While there is nothing wrong with this (do you really want to argue with an employer giving you more money?), it does affect how much you can deduct on your tax return. There is a limit on how much you can contribute to an HSA each year. For an individual plan (where only the employee is on the health plan), the contribution limit was $4,300 in 2025. For a family plan (where the employee and a spouse and/or child are on the plan), the contribution limit was $8,550 in 2025.[17]

However, you can only take a tax deduction for the amounts you *actually* contribute to the HSA (not what your employer gives). For example, if you have an individual plan and your employer contributes $2,000, you will only be able to contribute up to $2,300 in 2025. Your tax deduction, similarly, would be limited to $2,300.

---

17 Sec. 223(b)(3): If the employee is age fifty-five or older, an additional $1,000 may be contributed to an HSA each year.

What if both you and your spouse both have family plans? Can you contribute double? Unfortunately, no. While it is possible for each spouse to have their own HSA family plan, you can still only contribute up to the family plan limit when you combine your contributions.[18] Each spouse does not need to contribute equal amounts, as long as total contributions do not exceed the family plan limit. For example, one spouse contributing $5,000 to their family plan HSA and the other contributing $3,550 would be permissible in 2025 since total contributions do not exceed the family plan limit. However, each spouse contributing $8,550 to their own plan would not be allowed. If this were to happen, the additional contributions plus any earnings would need to be removed (otherwise, they would owe a 6 percent excise tax). HSA funds may be distributed tax-free as long as they are applied against any deductible medical expense (see the list of eligible medical expenses in Chapter 1). If distributions are made but *not* for medical expenses, you must pay a 20 percent penalty.

If you get sick a lot, you may want to stay away from an HSA. Remember that with an HSA, you have to have a high-deductible health plan. If you are often ill, you will be paying for these expenses out of pocket (since you need to meet your deductible amount). In this case, it may be better to just take another health plan. You won't be able to have an HSA, but you won't spend as much money out of pocket. HSAs work best for younger people who don't get sick very often—this gives the money in the HSA the best chance possible to grow tax-free and be there when you need it.

A major pro, though, is that you never really lose out on the money that accumulates in your HSA. If you retire, you can pull the money out tax-free once you reach age sixty-five. You don't have to use it for medical costs at that point. You can use it for any reason. Buy a Ferrari if you want to. After all, you are retired, right?

---

18 For example, consider a family of four. The spouses could each put one child on their health insurance plans, and both would be eligible for family plan coverage at their respective employers.

While HSAs do not have income limitations on deductibility, the amount may leave something to be desired. For example, in 2025, someone who qualifies for a family plan can only deduct up to $8,550 for HSA contributions. An $8,000 deduction is relatively small for someone who makes hundreds of thousands of dollars per year. It barely makes a dent. However, for a more moderate income level, this could be a huge deduction.

If you want to make a bigger impact (and you are self-employed), a Simplified Employee Pension (SEP) plan contribution may be the way to go. The contribution limits are much higher.[19]

Make a SEP Contribution

If you own your own business, you may have the option to contribute to a SEP IRA. A SEP is a retirement plan associated with a business. You can generally make contributions up until the due date of the tax return plus extensions (usually up until October 15 for a sole proprietorship).[20] You may contribute up to 25 percent of compensation or $70,000 (in 2025), whichever is less. If you are self-employed, you can contribute up to approximately 20 percent of your net income from self-employment—and deduct the whole thing! This is much higher than a contribution to a traditional IRA. Not to mention, you have much more time to make the contribution! You must make your contribution to a traditional IRA by April 15 to count it on your tax return for the year you are filing. However, with a SEP, you have all the way until October 15—the extended due date of the return.

But even with this flexibility and higher potential deduction, the SEP IRA does have some downsides. If you have employees, you generally need to include them in your SEP plan. Anti-discrimination

19 The SEP contribution limit in 2025 is $70,000.

20 If you have an S corporation or partnership, the extended due date of the business tax return would be September 15, not October 15.

rules say you cannot contribute to your own SEP plan without also contributing to your employees' SEP plans, too. (If you don't have employees, then this is obviously not a concern.) Also, you need to keep records of the tax year you made the contribution in, since custodians (like Schwab and Fidelity) are not required to keep track of the contribution's tax year.

Another complicating factor: Your business must show a profit for you to be able to take a SEP contribution deduction. Remember how we said you could contribute up to 20 percent of your net income (revenue minus expenses)? If you don't have any business income, you won't be able to contribute to a SEP. You could still contribute to an HSA or a traditional IRA, just not a SEP.

Despite the parameters, for those small business owners looking to lower their tax bill at the end of the year, though, a SEP contribution can have a huge impact. You can save on your tax bill and save some money for your retirement!

When Is a Penny Saved Not Really a Penny Earned?

So, what's the moral of the story? If you want to decrease your tax bill after the actual tax year is over, there are a few opportunities, as long as you don't mind doing things to benefit "future you." If you're willing to save for your future retirement or health needs, this strategy can work well.

But remember—these suggestions are not a dollar-for-dollar trade. In each of these cases (IRA, HSA, or SEP contribution), we are talking about tax deductions, not tax credits. While all of them will reduce the income subject to taxes, you will not save a dollar in taxes for every dollar you contribute to an IRA. You normally only save a fraction in actual tax money.

Let's assume you are in the 22 percent tax bracket and you currently owe $2,000 in taxes. If you contribute $1,000 to your HSA before April 15, you won't save $1,000 in taxes. You will only save $220 in taxes ($1,000 x 22% = $220). You will still need to send payment to the IRS for $1,780 ($2,000 - $220 = $1,780). Not to mention, you actually must make the $1,000 contribution to the HSA too! That means your cash flow out of pocket is actually higher ($1,000 HSA contribution + $1,780 tax bill = $2,000) than if you just paid the $2,000 to the IRS outright.

Is this a good deal? In general, I am a big fan of doing things to help future you as opposed to helping the government. (Yes, I am a selfish capitalist in that way!) Therefore, I am willing to pay a bit more to help me. However, if money is tight, this may be a tougher decision. Neither choice is bad. You just have to decide what is more important to you—keep the cash or pay a few dollars less in taxes and help future you.

Tips for Maximizing Savings: After the Tax Year is Over

1. If you qualify, traditional IRA contributions can be a great way to save some money on your tax return after the year is over. You generally have until April 15 to make a contribution.
2. HSAs are a great way to get some tax deductions and save toward future out-of-pocket healthcare expenses. The best part is that it doesn't matter how much money you make. Contributions to an HSA are always deductible, as long as you are in a high-deductible health plan.
3. For small business owners, SEP contributions provide the possibility for a very large tax deduction while also providing for sizable retirement savings.

CHAPTER 3

Side Gigs and Extra Income: What You Can Deduct

I am an entrepreneur at heart. I love seeing new ideas come to life when someone tries something on their own. I understand getting so caught up in an idea that you don't realize the implications right away of what you're doing. Perhaps that is why I'm so forgiving when someone comes to me after the year is over, flustered because they must decipher the tax implications of their new venture.

Side gigs like driving for Uber, delivering for Uber Eats, or performing services on TaskRabbit continue to gain popularity because they are easy ways to earn additional money, offer flexibility, and may even feed your entrepreneurial desires. After all, there is something exciting about trying something new and seeing if you can make a go of it!

From a tax perspective, the IRS generally treats most side gigs like running your own business. The same is true for anyone who works as a 1099 contractor, like many who hold part-time or project-based jobs as either their main or supplementary work. The good news is that this generally means you have a lot of deductions available. The bad news can be summed up in two words: self-employment taxes. Let's talk about both.

What Are Self-employment Taxes?

Whenever you run your own business or have a side gig, it's imperative to keep good accounting records. Regardless of whether your customers paid you by cash, check, credit card, or payment application, you need to declare all of it as revenue before taking your deductions.[21] As explained below, nearly all amounts paid that are ordinary, necessary, and reasonable are deductible for the business. Your total revenue minus your total deductions is your company's net income from self-employment. If you are the only owner of a business and you have not elected to be treated as a C corporation or S corporation, you will show the calculation of your net income (revenue minus deductions) on Schedule C on your personal income tax return.[22] Net income shown on Schedule C of your personal income tax return is subject to your regular income tax rate plus self-employment taxes.

If you have ever worked for an employer, take a look at your pay stub. On it, you will normally see two payroll taxes that have been taken out of your check—Social Security and Medicare taxes. Social Security taxes are calculated as 6.2 percent of your wages, while Medicare taxes are calculated at 1.45 percent of wages. Your employer pays a matching amount of payroll taxes on your wages equal to 6.2 percent of your wages for Social Security[23] and 1.45 percent for Medicare taxes. When

---

21 It's a common misconception that cash payments from customers do not need to be declared as income. All forms of payment, regardless of amount, must be declared as income on the tax return. See Sec. 61.

22 If you form an LLC, you can generally choose to be treated as a C corporation or an S corporation. If you make either of these elections, the business must file a separate tax return. In other words, the business will have its own tax return—and you will not be able to show the business income on your personal tax return.

23 Up to a certain amount of wages. The 6.2 percent tax is paid on the first $176,100 in wages in 2025. This amount of wages normally increases a bit each year due to inflation. Therefore, the amount of Social Security tax an employee pays is limited. This is not true of Medicare taxes, though. Medicare taxes do not have a wage base limit like Social Security taxes do!

you are self-employed, the IRS assumes you are both the employer and employee for the company. Therefore, you pay both the employer and employee sides of Social Security and Medicare taxes, totaling 15.3 percent (6.2% + 6.2% + 1.45% + 1.45% = 15.3%). This 15.3 percent tax, representing both the employer and employee side of Social Security and Medicare taxes, is collectively referred to as self-employment taxes.

Self-employment taxes are paid on the net income of the business in addition to your regular tax rate. If you don't have net income from your business, no self-employment taxes are owed. Therefore, self-employment taxes tend to sneak up on new business owners, as well as people who have just started a side gig. Once they start turning a profit from their venture, they have a bigger tax bill due to these pesky taxes!

What Can I Deduct?

The good news is that you can reduce your self-employment taxes by simply taking all deductions to which you're entitled. In my experience, when a client first starts a new business or side gig, they don't do a great job of keeping track of expenses. They forget about expenditures from earlier in the year. It could be helpful to keep a separate bank account for your business (that you run all business-related income and expenditures through) and keep track of everything in an accounting program or Excel file. You'll be making sure all deductions are easy to locate and calculate.

Because most businesses run on a cash basis, you are able to deduct your ordinary, necessary, and reasonable deductions as soon as you pay for them. Therefore, one way to keep your self-employment income to a minimum is to consider paying for a business expense during the year rather than waiting until the next year. For example, say your business needs office supplies soon. You may want to consider purchasing more in December of this year as opposed to waiting until January—so you can take the deductions in the current year rather than waiting. While there are some limitations around this[24], in general, the tax code allows you to "accelerate" deductions into the current year by paying for them in the current year.

The IRS generally allows you to deduct any business expense that is ordinary, necessary, and reasonable under the circumstances. While there are some expenses with additional requirements (more on that later), most business-related expenses are going to be deductible. The one requirement is to keep it reasonable for *your* business. For example, a hammer and screwdriver are probably deductible for a contractor, but not if you're an attorney. Similarly, cattle feed is deductible for a dairy farmer, but that same expenditure would likely not be available as a write-off to a plumber. All business expenses need to be reasonable under the circumstances for the given business.

There are a few things that go against this principle. For example, in nearly all instances, political contributions are not deductible. The same is true for fines and penalties assessed by the IRS against you because they would never be considered "ordinary or necessary" for any business. However, almost every other normal business expense is deductible.

One important thing: The IRS normally wants to see substantiation. For every deduction you take, you should be able to show you *actually* spent the money on something business-related. In most cases, this means keeping receipts, canceled checks, or credit card transaction records. You should also try to classify the expenses into the type of business expense it is, such as office supplies, inventory, or legal fees. This will help you recognize the business purpose of the expenditure. And if you are ever audited by the IRS, you'll have no problem showing them where the money went.

---

24 See the 12-month rule for prepaid expenses: Regs. Sec. 1.263(a)-4(f)(1)

Strict Substantiation? That Sounds Scary . . .

I have always been a rule follower. When I was a kid learning how to bake cupcakes for the first time, I remember meticulously following the recipe—convinced that if I messed up, the world would end and I would be shamefully scorned by every cupcake connoisseur. However, my classmates were less encumbered by how much of each ingredient was required. I remember my young grade school mind being appalled when a friend of mine simply threw in some additional sugar into the batter without measuring. He looked at me and shrugged. "Good enough," he said and moved on.

As I've gotten older, I now realize that not everything requires perfection. You can put in a bit more sugar into your cake batter, and the recipe will come out fine (even better sometimes). You can get away with some uneven strokes when painting your bedroom. You can even arrive at a meeting a few minutes late and no one really notices. However, this is not true for everything in this world. On the tax return, the IRS expects certain rules to be followed and items to be accurate to the dollar.

I am going to let you in on a secret. Are you ready for it? The IRS knows about all the business deductions people tend to "fudge" on. They know people occasionally exaggerate their business miles. They also know people tend to try to deduct meals that aren't actually related to business. They also know that some nefarious individuals might say something is a business travel expense when it was actually for a personal vacation!

In all seriousness, certain types of deductions are easy to manipulate. As a result, these are subject to "strict substantiation" rules. In other words, you can't deduct these things on your tax return unless you follow the documentation requirements to the letter. Probably the three most common deductions subject to strict substantiation requirements are business miles, business meals, and travel costs.[25] Let's look briefly at each.

Business Miles

In Tax Land, there are three different types of mileage: personal miles, commuting miles, and business miles. Out of the three, only business miles are deductible. While personal miles are generally any miles that don't fit in the other two categories, discerning between business miles and commuting miles is a bit more difficult. The drive from home to work, as well as the drive from work to home, are commuting miles. Once I am at the office, mileage to go see clients, run ordinary and necessary business errands, or attend education events are all considered to be business miles. Taxpayers usually can deduct either their business miles multiplied by a standard rate[26] or the actual expenses they incur using their vehicle.[27]

While this sounds simple, there are several important things to remember. First, even though the only deductible miles are business miles, the taxpayer needs to keep track of all three types. You can use an app or simply use a notebook and pen. Regardless of the record-keeping method you choose, you will need to declare how many miles you had in each category on the tax return (business, commuting, and

25 Technically, strict substantiation requirements are discussed in Sec. 274(d) and don't include business miles per se. However, in most cases, deductions related to business miles must be substantiated in a similar way as the other items discussed in Sec. 274(d). If you don't have the right elements in the business mileage log, the IRS will normally just deny the deduction!

26 The standard mileage rate normally changes each year due to inflation. In 2025, it is 70 cents per mile.

27 Only the business portion of vehicle expenses is deductible. So if you use your vehicle 50 percent of the time for business and 50 percent of the time for personal use, only half of your actual expenses are deductible.

personal[28]). For business miles, you should put together a log. The log should include the date, business miles traveled, and the purpose of the trip (attend client meeting, meet with business partner, and so on). Tracking commuting miles does not need to be done in a log, but one should generally know how long the trip is from home to work and work to home each day. Most people work about 250 days each year.[29] Take your average daily round trip to work each day and multiply it by 250, and this should be about what your commuting miles are for the year. Finally, personal miles may be tracked by simply looking at the odometer in your car at the beginning of the year and at the end of the year. If you subtract your beginning odometer reading from your ending odometer reading, this will give you the total miles you drove during the year. You then subtract out your commuting and business miles from this total, and these are your personal miles.

For example, say you subtract your beginning odometer reading from your ending reading and see that you drove 12,000 miles during the year. You kept a mileage log, so you know you had 3,000 business miles during the year. You also know you had 1,000 commuting miles. Therefore, your personal miles are 8,000 (12,000 - 3,000 - 1,000 = 8,000).

Second, aside from keeping a mileage log, you cannot estimate or "reconstruct" the log after the fact. The IRS generally wants you to keep the log throughout the year. Since business miles are subject to strict substantiation requirements, if a log cannot be produced to document the business mileage, the IRS may not allow the deduction.

Many taxpayers found this out during the pandemic. Even though many cities were shut down, bold taxpayers seeking to reduce their taxable income took large mileage deductions (often in round numbers, like 2,000 business miles or 3,000 business miles). The IRS was quick to

28 Technically, the tax return asks for "Other" miles. However, this is the same thing as personal miles since personal miles are not business miles.

29 This assumes someone works five days per week and fifty weeks out of the year. It assumes they take two weeks off for vacation.

send out letters asking for a business mileage log to support the deductions. The moral of the story: Don't guess and keep documentation!

Third, it is difficult (but not impossible) to have all business miles. In today's modern world, many people work from home. If you work from home and only use the car for business-related purposes, then you would have no commuting or personal miles. All miles would be business miles in this rare case. However, this is only possible if the person has a vehicle only used for business.

Fourth, be aware that certain professions have special rules regarding mileage. For example, if you are constantly traveling to different job sites or are a long-haul trucker, the rules are a bit different. For most everyone else, though, the rules above will apply!

Business Meals

Business meals are another area the IRS deems ripe for abuse. Therefore, only 50 percent of a business meal cost is deductible. Also, you must document who you meet with and the business purpose of the meal. It's important to keep your receipt showing the amount, time, and date. All of these elements are normally necessary to meet the strict substantiation requirements. If you're ever flagged by the IRS over business meal deductions, the agency will want to see documentation to justify your deduction.

Remember, all business deductions must generally be reasonable under the circumstances. In other words, avoid overly lavish meals. This doesn't mean you can't take a client out for a steak dinner, but too many extravagant meals may result in the IRS denying the deduction. Also, while sending someone a meal using a delivery service (such as Uber Eats, DoorDash, or Grubhub) became popular during the pandemic and can be a great gesture, you need to be present at the business meal for it to be deductible.[30] Remember, the reason why a business

30 This could potentially be a business gift, but the IRS places several limits around what may be deducted as a business gift as well.

meal is deductible is because there is a business element being discussed over the meal!

Finally, one thing that changed several years ago is that entertainment expenses are no longer deductible. While food and entertainment often go together when trying to impress clients, only 50 percent of the cost of the meals is generally deductible. If I decide to take a client out to a baseball game and pay for a hot dog lunch, only half of the cost of the hot dog lunch would be deductible. The cost of the ticket would not be deductible, nor the parking, nor any other entertainment costs. Always get a separate receipt for the meals portion so you can at least get a 50 percent deduction for that part![31]

Travel Costs

Even in a world where video conferencing is the norm, it is not unusual for someone to travel for business purposes. Strict substantiation requirements apply here too. Make sure you document the amount, time, place, and business purpose of each expense.[32] This might mean obtaining receipts from ridesharing services, hotel invoices, receipts from meals, and e-bills for airline tickets. Again, the point here (as with all of the items subject to strict substantiation) is to ensure you can prove the cost is a legitimate business expense. For this reason, it is also important to make sure the main purpose of the trip is business—not a personal vacation. If there are too many elements of personal pleasure, the deduction could be denied.

While there are a lot of potential pitfalls here, these deductions can be very valuable. For those who do a lot of driving for their job (delivery drivers, truck drivers, and so on), mileage deductions can result in huge tax savings. If you are a salesperson, meals with clients

31 In the case of an all-inclusive cost, everything is considered non-deductible. Only when the cost of meals can be separated and isolated from entertainment costs are meals 50 percent deductible.

32 Reg. 1.274-5A(b)(2)

and potential clients may be an integral part of your business. The key is just knowing how to document these deductions. If you do it right, then there are plenty of tax savings to be had!

Isn't There Anything Else I Can Do to Lower My Tax Bill on My Side Gig?

At this point, you might be wondering if a side hustle is still worth it! After all, you have to pay both self-employment taxes and regular income taxes. You also have to substantiate all deductions. Not to mention, you may struggle to find time to do it if you already have a full-time job! Is this really worth it?

Before you go deleting your Uber or DoorDash app, there are a few deductions that *only* the self-employed can take: self-employed health insurance deduction, home office deduction, and SEP deduction.

Self-Employed Health Insurance Deduction

Remember that a side gig is generally looked at by the IRS as being the same as a business. Therefore, if you don't have health insurance through your employer (or your spouse's employer), you may qualify for a self-employed health insurance deduction. Say you must buy health insurance coverage through the marketplace. You will generally be able to deduct your health insurance premium, as well as any long-term care insurance premiums you pay out of pocket. Alternatively, say you're retired but want something to do. You decided to take on a side gig. Any Medicare premiums you pay would be deductible as well.

There are some limits to pay attention to. First, you can take a self-employed health insurance deduction to the extent that you actually had a profit for your business on Schedule C (or Schedule F).[33] Let's say you paid $4,000 for health insurance premiums, but your side gig only generated $1,000 in income. Your deduction would generally be limited to $1,000.[34] Second, the amount of long-term care insurance premiums you can deduct is limited by your age. For 2025, the maximum amounts you can deduct for long-term care insurance premiums are:

- Age 40 or younger: $480
- Age 41 to 50: $900
- Age 51 to 60: $1,800
- Age 61 to 70: $4,810
- Age 71 or older: $6,020

Remember, you cannot take the deduction for any month you were covered under a plan through your employer or your spouse's employer.[35] Also, the self-employed health insurance deduction will only reduce your regular income taxes; it will *not* reduce your self-employment taxes. But even with these limitations, this can be a lucrative deduction, though, if you don't have coverage through another source.

Home Office Deduction

---

33 You can also take the deduction if: a) You were a partner with net earnings from self-employment for the year reported on Schedule K-1 (Form 1065), box 14, code A; b) You used one of the optional methods to figure your net earnings from self-employment on Schedule SE; or c) You received wages in 2023 from an S corporation in which you were a more-than-2-percent shareholder. Health insurance premiums paid or reimbursed by the S corporation are shown as wages on Form W-2.

34 Form 7206 also has some additional limitations. Our purpose here is to simply show that if you don't have any self-employment income, you cannot take the deduction.

35 You also can't take the deduction if you were covered under your dependent's plan. Additionally, there are some limitations for retired public safety officers.

Several years ago, many people qualified for a home office deduction. However, after the Tax Cuts and Jobs Act provisions became effective in 2018, the home office deduction is only available to self-employed individuals. Again, since the IRS looks at a side gig as the equivalent of being self-employed, you might be eligible for a home office deduction too.

Like so many other things in Tax Land, there are limitations on the deduction. As discussed with the self-employed health insurance deduction, you generally need to have income from your side gig in order to take this deduction. Also, there are two different ways to calculate the deduction—the simplified method and the actual expense method. Under the simplified method, you take the square footage of your home office and multiply it by $5 per square foot to calculate your deduction. The most you can deduct is $1,500. For example, if my home office is 200 square feet, my deduction will be $1,000 (200 x $5 = $1,000). If my home office were 350 square feet, though, I would only be able to take $1,500 as a deduction (350 square feet x $5 = $1,750, but the most you can deduct is $1,500). The simplified method works pretty well if you don't like keeping track of a lot of invoices. All you need is a tape measure to measure your office (and possibly a calculator)!

The actual expense method is a bit more time-consuming, but it can result in a much larger deduction. Essentially, you take a portion of all of the actual expenses of the house as a deduction without having to worry about the $1,500 deduction limit. For example, say the square footage of your home is 3,000 square feet, and the square footage of your home office is only 300 square feet. In this instance, you can deduct 10 percent of the actual expenses of your home as a home office deduction (300 / 3,000 = 10%). This means you can generally take 10 percent of any of the following:

- Mortgage interest
- Insurance
- Home utilities

- Real estate taxes
- General home repairs

You could also take a deduction for depreciation, as well as 100 percent of any expenses for the home office. If you had to patch a hole in the ceiling of the home office, this would actually be 100 percent deductible. You get to deduct the entire cost of items directly related to the home office and a percentage of any indirect expenses. This could be a very lucrative deduction! However, remember—you can only take a home office deduction if you are using that office for your side gig, and only to the extent that your side gig is profitable! Unlike the self-employed health insurance deduction, the home office deduction will reduce both self-employment taxes and regular income taxes.

SEP Contribution Deduction

We discussed the SEP contributions earlier in this book. If you are self-employed or have a side gig, you can make a SEP contribution as well. The amount of the SEP contribution depends on how much money you make from your side gig. Also, if you have a retirement plan through your employer, you may be limited on how much you can contribute to a SEP plan. For example, say you work for an employer and you have a 401(k), but you also have a side gig. The amount of your contributions to your SEP may be reduced depending on how much has been contributed to your 401(k) during the year by you and your employer.

In spite of this potential complication, a SEP can be a great way to reduce your tax bill. Similar to the self-employed health insurance deduction, though, it will not reduce your self-employment taxes—only your regular income taxes.

Can I Pay Myself and Reduce My Business Income (and Self-employment Taxes)?

This is a hard question. Some entity types do not allow for wages to be paid. Most side gigs will generally be considered sole proprietorships. In a sole proprietorship, the owner cannot be paid wages. Self-employment taxes will be assessed on any net income the company earns. This is also true of a single-member LLC (a limited liability company with one owner) and a partnership (or an LLC with more than one business owner).[36]

If you formalize your side gig into an S corporation or C corporation, then you can pay yourself—but your compensation needs to be reasonable. This generally means it needs to be what you would get paid on the open market, no more and no less. You may deduct these amounts, which will reduce your company income. Self-employment taxes are generally not assessed against S or C corporation net income.[37]

You can change your entity type, but generally, once you pick an entity type, you are stuck with it for at least five years. If you are not formed as a sole proprietorship or single-member LLC, you will have to file a separate tax return, make filings with the Secretary of State, and have other administrative costs. The decision to formalize your business into one of these other entity types is not one to take lightly! Still, paying yourself *is* possible as long as you have the right structure—and your compensation is comparable to those in your industry with the same level of experience.

---

36 With a partnership, it may be possible to pay yourself a guaranteed payment. However, guaranteed payments are generally subject to self-employment taxes.

37 It is important to remember that the company will pay payroll taxes on any wages that you pay yourself.

Will My Tax Preparer Charge Me More If I Have a Side Gig?

Most of the time, the answer to this question is yes. While every tax preparer is different, nearly all of them will price a return higher if they need to put more time into it. As mentioned, most side gigs will be shown on Schedule C of your personal tax return. Schedule C is complicated, and your preparer will want to ensure all income and deductions are properly accounted for. This takes time. In the heart of tax season, especially, your tax preparer's time is precious!

If you want to save some money, be well-organized. Don't just hand your preparer a box of receipts. Delivering all receipts, totaled and organized, can save your preparer precious minutes (or even hours) of time. This generally means a lower bill for you (and a much happier tax preparer)!

Tips for Maximizing Savings: Side Hustles

1. Remember, the IRS treats side gigs basically like self-employed businesses. Keep track of your business income and expenses throughout the year. Keep a separate checking account for your side gig so you can easily see both income and expenses for the year. If that's not possible, track everything in a separate spreadsheet or an accounting app.
2. Remember, items you buy for your side gig are deductible in the year you pay for them. This is known as the cash basis of accounting.[38] Consider paying for some items in December that

38 It is possible to have an accrual basis side gig, but this would be pretty rare.

you will use shortly after the new year, so you can accelerate those deductions into the current year.

3. The home office deduction, self-employed health insurance deduction, and SEP contribution deduction may be available if you have a side hustle. However, while all three reduce regular income taxes, only the home office deduction will reduce self-employment taxes as well.

CHAPTER 4

College Costs: Tax Tips for Sending a Kid to School

Perhaps nothing causes more panic to parents than sending a kid to college. Don't get me wrong. Most are happy to see their children seek to fulfill their dreams and career goals. They take pride in seeing how independent they are and how far they've come. If they are going to the same school as the parent, they may also reminisce about fond memories of first starting school. However, positive feelings can often turn to uneasiness when parents take a hard look at how much it will cost. More than one parent has looked at me with that "deer in headlights" expression and asked: "How in the world am I going to pay for this?"

I can't say I blame them. After all, according to an article by Forbes, the average cost of college has risen a whopping 180 percent over the last forty years.[39] The increase can be attributed to many factors, including colleges offering more student support services, the overall cost of living increasing, and higher demand overall. It's also true that increased faculty costs contribute to this number. Many students want

39 McGurran, Brianna. "College Tuition Inflation: Compare the Cost of College Over Time." *Forbes Advisor*, 9 May 2023.

faculty members with real-world experience, and this demand causes colleges to compete with real-world employers. After all, if an experienced teacher can make more money working in the private industry than for a college or university, why wouldn't they? Regardless of the reasons, the costs of higher education continue to skyrocket. Funding college continues to be a huge hurdle for many families.

The good news is that there are financially savvy ways to make that investment for your child. These strategies use key tax incentives—and sidestep the most common misconceptions along the way.

Understanding the FAFSA

For most colleges and universities, the starting point for determining whether a student is eligible for financial aid is the Free Application for Federal Student Aid (FAFSA). Once a student fills out the FAFSA, the school will use the form to determine what type of aid may be available to the student. Based on the FAFSA, the school may offer the student need-based scholarships, grants, or work-study opportunities.

The FAFSA itself utilizes a formula to determine need based on income and assets, including savings. That said, there is a major misconception that catches many families by surprise. Many families are surprised to learn the calculation is often based on both the child's *and* parents' income. The FAFSA makes a distinction between those students who are dependents and those who are independent. A student's income will only be considered if they are independent. Otherwise, the income of both the parent and the child will be counted. To determine whether a student is independent, the FAFSA asks ten questions. If the student answers yes to any of them, they are considered independent:

1. Will you be twenty-four or older by January 1 of the school year for which you are applying for financial aid? For example, if you plan to start school in August 2022 for the 2022–23 school year,

will you be twenty-four by January 1, 2022 (i.e., were you born before January 1, 1999)?

2. Are you married or separated but not divorced?
3. Will you be working toward a master's or doctorate degree (such as an MA, MBA, MD, JD, PhD, or EdD)?
4. Do you have children who receive more than half of their support from you?
5. Do you have dependents (other than children or a spouse) who live with you and receive more than half of their support from you?
6. Are you currently serving on active duty in the US armed forces for purposes other than training?
7. Are you a veteran of the US armed forces?
8. At any time since you turned age thirteen, were both of your parents deceased, were you in foster care, or were you a ward or dependent of the court?
9. Are you an emancipated minor or are you in a legal guardianship as determined by a court?
10. Are you an unaccompanied youth who is homeless or self-supporting and at risk of being homeless?

As a result, many students will be unable to claim independent status even if they are making a small amount of income. Need will often be based on both the parents' and the child's income—which may result in the child qualifying for far less financial aid.

This reality can inform the financial decisions you make just before and while sending your kid to college. Since most of the information needed for the FAFSA comes directly from the tax return, it is important to control taxable income in years where dependents are in college (and therefore are going to be filling out the FAFSA). For example, don't take money out of a retirement account during those years because this will lower your taxable income. If you can push off your bonus to a future period, that can help as well. Also, try not to sell appreciated investments in those years. All of these techniques help keep your income low—and increase the chances for you or your family member to receive the most financial aid possible.

Deducting Student Loan Interest

The weight of student loan debt can feel crushing. The interest on those loans seems to add insult to injury. But if you have it, you may as well see what you can do with it. Student loan interest can be deducted on a tax return up to $2,500 per year, as long as you are not claimed as a dependent.[40] Also, in order to take advantage of the deduction, you need to be responsible for the loan itself. A parent generally cannot take a deduction for a loan that their child is responsible for; they can only take a deduction for loans they are responsible for.

Unfortunately, that $2,500 is the limit. *What if I pay $10,000 in student loan interest on an education loan? Surely, I can deduct more, right?* Nope. *That amount must go up with inflation each year, right?* Nope. It is $2,500—and it has been for a long time, even though student loan interest rates have generally increased. While this may not be very much for higher-income earners, it can be meaningful for lower-income earners.

In order to deduct student loan interest, you'll also need to make sure you don't surpass the income limit. In 2025, if you are married, the phaseout is from $170,000 to $200,000 ($85,000 to $100,000 if you are single). This means that if you and your spouse have a modified adjusted gross income (MAGI) of $200,001, you will receive no deduction for your student loan interest. The only way that you are able to get the full $2,500 is if you have MAGI of $170,000 or less if you are married. Please keep in mind that tax law changes all the time. These

40 Sec. 221(b)(1).

are the numbers for 2025. They may have changed by the time you get done reading this sentence!

Make no mistake: Student loan debt and the interest accrued is not "good debt"—for you or your child. That said, if you can take advantage of the tax deduction, you may be able to save meaningfully on your taxes.

Differentiating Taxable vs. Tax-Free Scholarships

A scholarship may or may not be tax-free depending on what it is used for and what (if anything) needs to be done to obtain the scholarship. You may apply to either type, as a scholarship can have major benefits even if it is not tax-free. However, knowing the difference will better set you up for your education funding plan.

Scholarships are generally tax-free for the student if used to cover tuition, mandatory fees, books, supplies, and equipment required for courses of instruction. However, if scholarships are used to cover other expenses, like room and board, they are taxable income. Excess scholarships may arise from overly generous financial aid packages. While many students are grateful for the money (especially if they are attending a school in a high-cost-of-living area), some may be surprised to see their tax bill in April!

A second consideration is whether the scholarship money comes with any conditions. For example, if a scholarship requires the student to do research or other work for the school or organization that awarded it, the scholarship is considered the equivalent to compensation. Think about it. The student is providing services in exchange for something of value (the cost of education at the school). Does this arrangement sound familiar? If this situation reminds you of your agreement with your employer, then you can certainly understand the

IRS's position. The IRS treats such "scholarships" like any other form of compensation: taxable income and reported on a Form W-2. What if the scholarship is awarded to a student by an organization and the only requirement is that the student spend a few hours each month traveling around the country telling the public how great the organization is? Unfortunately, that scholarship will probably also be taxable.

To be treated as a tax-free scholarship, the IRS requires detached and disinterested generosity only to be used toward certain expenses described above. To avoid unwelcome surprises on the tax return, review scholarship requirements and what the scholarship covers as your child applies.

Remember: Assuming a scholarship qualifies to be tax-free, it can only benefit the student. The student receives the scholarship and does not have to declare the money as gross income on their tax return. And since many parents pay their child's tax liabilities while they are in school, a tax break for your student child is a tax break for you!

Contributing to a 529 Plan

Section 529 plans have grown in popularity as the cost of college has increased. These are tax-advantaged plans used to save for education, administered by each individual state. Funds that are contributed to a 529 plan are invested in the markets and (assuming the markets do well) increase in value over time. Funds may be pulled from the account tax-free, as long as they are used toward the cost of attending a college or university.

The 529 plan is an excellent tool for tax-free growth! If you were to just save for a college fund using a taxable brokerage account that you opened with a financial adviser, you would pay taxes on any capital gains, interest income, or dividends the account generates. If the funds are inside a 529 plan, none of these same items are taxable. Therefore, the funds can grow faster (if the markets cooperate)—and more college costs can be paid for when the time comes!

You can use up to $10,000 of 529 plan funds to pay for kindergarten through twelfth-grade tuition as well. To get the most tax savings and flexibility possible from a 529 plan, it may be best to open one when the child is young (even when they are first born).

Keep in mind that 529 plan fund distributions are not taxable—*if* the funds are used to pay for education. However, that doesn't mean that every single expense a college student may incur can be paid for using 529 plan money. The Internal Revenue Code says the following items may be paid for using 529 plan money, tax-free:[41]

- Tuition, fees, books, supplies, and equipment.
- Expenses incurred for special needs services for a special needs beneficiary.
- Expenses for the purchase of computer or peripheral equipment, computer software, or internet access and related services if it's to be used primarily by the beneficiary during any of the years the beneficiary is enrolled at an eligible educational institution.
- Room and board expenses incurred by an eligible student who is attending an eligible educational institution at least half-time.[42]

Notice what is listed here, as well as what isn't. If you use 529 plan money to pay for your kid to travel home over the holidays, this would be a taxable distribution. However, paying for eligible student housing using 529 plan money would be tax-free. If you do happen to pay for something using 529 plan money that is not an eligible expense (like travel expenses), the earnings on the account will be subject to a 10 percent penalty in addition to regular income taxes.

---

41 Sec. 529(f)(1).

42 There is a limitation on the amount of room and board that may be paid for with 529 plan funds (see Sec. 529((e)(3)(B)(ii)).

Lastly, be aware that these contributions are not totally tax-deductible—and may not be deductible at all. There is no deduction available on the *federal* tax return for contributions to a 529 plan. Several *states* offer a tax deduction. For example, at the time of this writing, the Commonwealth of Virginia offers a deduction of up to $4,000 on the Virginia income tax return. Other states, like North Carolina, do not. Still, a 529 plan is an opportunity well worth exploring for anyone funding an education.

Utilizing Education Tax Credits

Perhaps the biggest opportunity available for those funding an education is in the form of two education tax credits—the American Opportunity Tax Credit (AOTC) and the Lifetime Learning Credit (LLC).

A tax credit is different from a tax deduction. The terms are similar but far from the same. A deduction (what some people call a write-off) is a reduction in the amount of income that is subject to taxation. A tax credit, on the other hand, is a dollar-for-dollar reduction in your tax liability.

For example, if you are in the 20 percent tax bracket and you have $10,000 of taxable income on your tax return, your tax liability is $2,000 ($10,000 taxable income x 20% = $2,000 taxes due). A $1,000 tax deduction would make your taxable income only $9,000. Therefore, your tax liability would be $1,800 ($9,000 remaining taxable income x 20% = $1,800 taxes due).

Now, imagine you still owe $2,000 in taxes, but instead of a $1,000 deduction, you have a $1,000 tax credit. A $1,000 tax credit would make it so your tax liability would only be $1,000 ($2,000 taxes due before the credit - $1,000 tax credit = $1,000 remaining taxes due). While the $1,000 deduction only saved you $200, the $1,000 credit saved you the full $1,000! Tax credits are much more valuable than tax deductions.

The AOTC and the LLC were created to benefit different types of students. For those attending undergraduate college or university, either may be used—but the AOTC is often best. For those attending graduate school, the LLC is usually the only option. We'll explore each to see if either can help you with putting your kid through college.

American Opportunity Tax Credit (AOTC)

The AOTC is a tax credit of up to $2,500 available during each of the first four years of college only. In order to receive the full $2,500 credit, you need to pay tuition and required expenses of at least $4,000. In other words, it generally only applies to undergraduate education, but if you're helping pay for your kid's school, this is likely exactly what you need. To qualify for the credit, the student has to be enrolled at least half-time. Most colleges and universities have a certain number of credits you must take to be considered half-time. For example, a college may say you must take at least six semester credits to be considered half-time.[43] The student must also be working toward a degree rather than taking classes à la carte.[44]

The credit may be taken when expenses like tuition and mandatory fees are paid for the student out of pocket. The credit cannot be taken on the following expenses:

- Room and board
- Insurance
- Medical expenses (including student health fees)

---

43 Sec. 25A(b)(2)(B).

44 The credit cannot be claimed by a married filing separately taxpayer, a foreign person (a non-resident alien), or anyone who has been convicted of a felony drug offense—see Sec. 25A(g)(6), Sec 25A(g)(7), and Sec 25A(b)(2)(D).

- Transportation
- Similar personal, living, or family expenses

Also, note that the credit can only be taken when a client spends money *out of pocket*. In other words, if you paid for the expense using scholarship money or 529 plan funds, you cannot take a credit for it. However, if you paid for it with student loan funds or your own personal savings, you *can* take the tax credit. The credit is taken on your federal tax return by filing Form 8863.

What can be confusing is who can take the credit: the student or the parent? It is generally only when the student can be claimed as a dependent that the credit may be claimed by the parent. If the student is not a dependent, then only the student can claim the credit.

Lifetime Learning Credit (LLC)

While AOTC is great for those in undergraduate programs, it doesn't help a student with graduate school costs. And those are more expensive! So, what can a graduate student or someone going back to school for a second bachelor's degree do? Enter the Lifetime Learning Credit.

The LLC isn't worth as much as the AOTC. An AOTC can be taken for up to $2,500, but the LLC is only available for up to $2,000. However, it does offer several advantages over the AOTC. First, one can take an LLC even if they are just enrolled in a few classes. Your student doesn't have to be enrolled at least half-time, like you do with the AOTC. This is especially useful for graduate students who are only able to attend school part-time due to work, family commitments, or other obligations. Second, the student does not have to be enrolled in a degree program. They could just want to shore up their skills in a certain area—and this qualifies for the LLC.

My dad has owned his own business for several years. At one point, he decided he was tired of paying someone else to do the bookkeeping and went back to school to take some accounting classes. He was not seeking a degree in accounting, and he did not have time to go to school full-time; he only wanted to take a class or two at night to gain the skills necessary to help his business. Situations like this are perfect for the LLC. The student can take a class or two and still take up to $2,000 off their tax bill!

Like the AOTC, the LLC can only be taken when you spend money on education costs (see list above). The LLC is also calculated a bit differently, so you need to have at least $10,000 of education expenses before you can actually get the full $2,000 credit.[45] However, to a graduate student working hard to make ends meet, the LLC can provide some much-needed relief! Additionally, while the AOTC is limited to the first four years of post-secondary education, there is no limit to the number of years you can claim the LLC. If you need a bit more time to get through your graduate program, that's not a problem for the LLC!

So, what's the catch? Similar to the student loan interest deduction, there is a phaseout applicable to the AOTC and the LLC. Again, if you make too much money, then these credits may not be available to you. For 2025, a married taxpayer may only take the maximum amount for either credit if they have income of $160,000 or less. Once they have an income of $180,000, neither credit is available.[46]

Like the AOTC, the Lifetime Learning Credit is only generally available to the parent if the child is claimed as a dependent. If the child is not claimed, only the child can take the credit.

45 The credit is calculated as 20 percent of the first $10,000 of qualified expenses.

46 For single taxpayers, the phaseout is half of these limits. Only when a single taxpayer's MAGI is $80,000 or below can they qualify for the maximum credit. The credit phases out completely once MAGI reaches $90,000.

What If I Want to Continue My Own Education?

While the focus of this chapter has been on putting a child through college, each of these strategies applies if your goal is to continue your own education.

You can open a 529 plan for yourself, your spouse, or any dependents. While many people open them for children, this is certainly not their only use. It may be good to open one if you know you want to go to college or obtain a graduate degree!

Tips for Maximizing Savings: Putting a Kid Through College

1. If a child can qualify as independent (that is, not your dependent), it can be best for the family. If a child pays for their own college expenses, they may be able to take one of the education credits or the student loan interest deduction. Parents often make too much money to take advantage of these incentives—but let's face it, college kids are usually making very little money (which gives them a better chance to take advantage of some of these tax incentives).
2. If your income level qualifies you for the student loan interest deduction or tax credits, take advantage of these on your tax return. The AOTC tax credit will likely be the most applicable credit if you're funding a child's undergraduate schooling.
3. If you make too much money to take advantage of the tax credits or the loan interest deduction, invest more into a 529 plan. You can start one when your child is young and take advantage of that tax-free growth, no matter how much money you make! This account can be used for K–12 education as well as college.

CHAPTER 5

From Diapers to Deductions: Tax Breaks for Raising Kids

The woman let out an audible grunt as she took another foot to the stomach. Then, she felt a wet hand slap her across the face, knocking her glasses crooked. She turned up her nose, bracing herself for a knee she anticipated hitting her chin. Was she an MMA fighter? No. A boxer? No. A professional wrestler? No. She was just a mom in my office trying to read and sign off on her tax return while her young daughter attempted to climb her like a mountaineer reaching the summit.

"I realize your daughter doesn't know me. But do you think she would come to me just for a second?" She was only two years old, but she never seemed to stop moving. She was in a constant state of motion—ready to explore the world!

"Yes!" The mom said, relieved as she thrust her in my direction.

I took the child and distracted her for all of about four seconds by making funny faces and showing her my keys.

"Dave, kids are great—but expensive. There has to be a tax break here, right?" My client had signed off on her return and was now enjoying a free moment before resuming the endless wrestling match.

"There are plenty of deductions and credits available for kids," I said as a small foot pressed into my gut. The entertainment of my keys had worn off, and now her daughter had decided to climb me instead.

"I know it may not be much, but every dollar helps. We spend money on formula, diapers, and lots of stuff for her. It does help!"

I've had countless conversations like this. The economic realities of having a new child hit parents, and they wonder what they can do. The good news is, there are some tax incentives available for parents. You just need to know what you are looking for!

Is My Kid a Dependent?

One thing that we need to get straight right off the bat is that not every child is a dependent. Tax incentives are generally given if you have a dependent—not just for merely having a child. At a certain point, normally due to age, a child is no longer your dependent. They will be able to take more of their own deductions, and you won't be able to take them anymore on your return. In short, kids grow up—when they do, the tax incentives stop. So, when is your kid considered a dependent? There are actually two ways to qualify: either as a qualifying child or a qualifying relative. Let's look at the rules for both.

Qualifying Child

To be considered a qualifying child, the dependent must meet *all* of the following tests[47]:

- *Dependent Taxpayer Test*: In general, you cannot be someone else's dependent and also claim a dependent on your own tax return. Said another way, if I am someone else's kid, I can't claim my own kid!

47 Sec. 152

- *Joint Return Test*: A dependent cannot file a joint tax return for him or herself and be claimed as a dependent on someone else's return. In other words, your kid can't file a joint tax return and then still be claimed by you.[48]
- *Citizen or Resident Test*: The child must be a US citizen or resident of the United States, Canada, or Mexico.
- *Relationship Test*: You can only claim as a dependent anyone who is:
- Son, daughter, stepchild, eligible foster child, adopted child, or a descendant (for example, your grandchild) of any of them, or
- Brother, sister, half brother, half sister, stepbrother, stepsister, or a descendant of any of them.
- *Age Test*: Your dependent must be:
- Under age nineteen at the end of the year and younger than you (or your spouse if filing jointly); or
- A full-time student under age twenty-four at the end of the year, and younger than you (or your spouse if filing jointly); or
- Permanently and totally disabled at any time during the year, regardless of age.
- *Residency Test*: In general, the child needs to live with you more than half of the year. Don't worry about temporary absences for school, vacation, or military service. Those don't count.
- *Support Test*: If the child pays for most of their own expenses (more than 50 percent), you cannot claim them.

All these tests must be met before you can claim your kid on the tax return. If you don't meet even one of these tests, your dependent is

---

48 Actually, if your child files a joint tax return only to claim a refund for the tax they have had withheld during the year, then you can still claim them. But this is going to be a rare exception! (Sec. 152(b)(2))

not a qualifying child. They could then only be claimed if they were a qualifying relative.

Qualifying Relative

Families come in many different shapes and sizes. If you are unable to claim someone as a qualifying child, you might be able to claim them as a qualifying relative. Like the qualifying child rules, though, you have to meet *all* the tests to claim them.

- *Dependent Taxpayer Test*: This rule is the same as above. If your child can claim their own dependents, you can no longer claim them as your dependent.
- *Joint Return Test*: Same as above. A dependent cannot file a joint tax return for him or herself and be claimed as a dependent on someone else's return. In other words, the child can't file a joint tax return and then still be claimed by you.[49]
- *Citizen or Resident Test*: Same as above. To be claimed, your dependent must be a US citizen or a resident of the United States, Canada, or Mexico.
- *Not a Qualifying Child Test*: If the dependent is a qualifying child, they cannot also be a qualifying relative. This is a bit redundant, because remember, the child just needs to qualify as one or the other. If they qualify as a qualifying child or a qualifying relative, then they are a dependent.
- *Member of Household/Relationship Test*: There are two ways to meet this test. 1.) Your dependent lives in your household for the entire year, or 2.) They are related to you in one of the following ways (even if they don't live with you):

---

49 Actually, if your child files a joint tax return only to claim a refund for the tax they have had withheld during the year, you can still claim them. But this is a rare exception! (Sec. 152(b)(2))

- Child or a descendant of a child.
- Brother, sister, stepbrother, or stepsister.
- Father or mother, or an ancestor of either.
- Stepfather or stepmother.
- Son or daughter of a brother or sister of the taxpayer.
- Brother or sister of the father or mother of the taxpayer.
- Son-in-law, daughter-in-law, father-in-law, mother-in-law, brother-in-law, or sister-in-law.
- *Gross Income Test*: Your dependent cannot have gross income over $5,200 (in 2025) and be claimed as a qualifying relative.
- *Support Test*: You must have paid for more than half of someone's expenses for them to meet this test.

Is It over yet? What Does This All Mean?

When I go into the details of the dependency rules with clients, I often have to wake them up at the end. These rules are intense, no doubt about it!

Here's the point: Don't assume just because someone is in your household, they can be taken as a dependent. Sometimes they can't. Once a child is out of school and working, for example, they normally can't be claimed (even if you are still washing their socks for them or packing their lunch). Sometimes college-age children may not qualify as well. However, if your kid is still living at home and you are supporting them (and they are not making too much money for themselves), you might be able to claim them as a qualifying relative. This also might be the case for an elderly parent whom you are supporting yourself; you could claim that elderly parent as a dependent.[50]

Tax Advantages for Having a Dependent

Many tax incentives are based on dependency. If you have dependents, you have the opportunity to take advantage of them. Before we discuss how you can do this, remember the difference between a tax credit and a tax deduction. A tax credit will reduce your tax bill dollar for dollar. A $5,000 credit will reduce your tax bill by $5,000. However, a deduction only reduces the income you pay taxes on. Credits are normally more valuable than deductions. When it comes to kids, there are some credits and some deductions.

Child Tax Credit

You can usually take a $2,200 child tax credit for each of your dependents under age seventeen.[51] The credit is per child, so if you have more than one child, you can get more than one credit.

While this is a nice little bonus for most families, the credit does go away if your income is too high. If you make more than $400,000 and are married, or $200,000 and are single, the credit phases out. [52] These limits are pretty high, though, so many people take advantage of this credit.

---

50 It should be noted that you can't have dependents if you are a dependent. So, for example, if your child has a child (your grandchild) that they can claim as a dependent on their return, you cannot claim your child as a dependent.

51 This information is up to date as of 2025.

52 The $200,000 and $400,000 are AGI limits.

If your dependent(s) are seventeen years or older, you can take a credit of $500 per dependent. While this is less, it is certainly a nice bonus!

Child & Dependent Care Credit

My mother did full-time daycare out of my house when I was a kid. There were always kids in my room when I would get home from school. While this annoyed me at times (especially when they got into my Transformers action figures), I was always amazed at how much the parents would thank my mom whenever they'd pick up their kids at the end of the workday. I distinctly remember one mother crying as she told my mother how much she meant to her.

As I have grown older, I understand this a bit better now. If parents are going to work, they need somewhere for their children to go during the day. Even if they are in school, they need a safe place to go afterward. These places are not cheap either. My house growing up was a safe place for kids—and my mom didn't charge as much as the other centers in the area. Many of the kids and I were close friends, and my mom wanted to help them and their families out.

Whether you take your kids to a daycare center or to a provider like my mom, you may be able to take a tax credit between $600 and $2,100. The actual amount will vary depending on how much money you make and whether you have one or more children. If you make more money, you will be toward the lower end of the credit (closer to the $600 range for one child or $1,200 for two or more). To qualify for this credit, however, the child must be your dependent. Again, it all starts with dependency! But for those who can claim a dependent, these savings can make a huge difference.

Earned Income Credit (EIC)

The EIC is a tax credit available for lower-income taxpayers. While it's possible to claim the EIC without children, it doesn't happen often. Also, if you have more children, you are normally able to take advantage of a higher credit amount. For 2025, here are the maximum credit amounts that may be taken:

- No qualifying children: $649
- 1 qualifying child: $4,328
- 2 qualifying children: $7,152
- 3 or more qualifying children: $8,046

Again, the EIC is only available to lower-income taxpayers. In other words, once you start making too much money, you will be unable to access it. For 2024, the credit is reduced if you have income (AGI) above the threshold phaseout. You can no longer take the credit at all if you are above the completed phaseout amount (AGI) shown below:

<IRS Table Showing EIC Tax Credit maximum amounts for 2025>

Note that if you have investment income above $11,600, you also may not take the EIC.

What's the bottom line? If you are a lower-income taxpayer who works and has kids, you can take advantage of the EIC. If not, you will need to try to take advantage of the other opportunities we mention in this chapter!

Head of Household Filing Status

In the opening chapter of this book, we discussed taking a standard deduction versus itemizing deductions. Remember, you can take either one—just not both. The standard deduction is different depending on which filing status you choose. Here are the standard deduction amounts for 2025:

- Single or Married Filing Separately: $15,750
- Married Filing Jointly or Qualifying Surviving Spouse: $31,500
- Head of Household: $23,625

Notice that you receive a higher standard deduction if you file as head of household. To do so, you generally need to meet all the following requirements:

- You are not married.
- You pay over half of the expenses for the household for the year.
- You have a dependent who lives with you for more than six months out of the year.

Therefore, if you have a dependent, you may be able to file as head of household, allowing you to take a slightly higher standard deduction than if you filed as single. However, remember—the standard deduction only matters if you don't itemize. If you have itemized deductions (medical expenses, mortgage interest, taxes, and charitable contributions) that equal a greater amount than the standard deduction, you would itemize even if you qualify for head of household status.

What does this all mean? If you are a single parent who supports your kid, you can get a little bit higher standard deduction—and maybe shave a few dollars from your tax bill!

Medical Expenses

In the opening chapter, we discussed the types of medical expenses considered deductible. If you pay for your dependent's medical expenses, you can take an itemized deduction for the amounts you pay. Remember, only when you pay for medical expenses for yourself, your spouse, or your dependents are they deductible. Also, only medical expenses that are paid out of pocket are deductible. In other words, if a medical expense is reimbursed by insurance, you can't take a deduction for it.

From the time they are born until they go off to college, kids will need to go to the doctor, receive flu shots, and maybe even get braces. If you do end up paying for these things, you might as well take a tax deduction for them!

Do Kids Have to File Their Own Tax Returns?

Many parents are surprised to hear that kids *do* need to file their own tax returns if they have more than a certain amount of income:

- If a dependent child made more than $15,750 in earned income (wages or self-employment income) only in 2025, they need to file a tax return. They are over the standard deduction amount, so they may owe tax.
- If they made money only from their investments (dividends, interest, and capital gains), they need to file a tax return if this amount is more than $1,350 in 2025.
- If they made money from both earned income *and* investments, they would need to file a tax return if they are above the dependent standard deduction. The dependent standard deduction is earned income plus $450 in 2025 (not to exceed $15,750).

As you can see, the actual requirements are complicated. However, even if your child does not *need* to file a tax return, it may be beneficial. Why? At the very least, they can get their withholding back. Let's say your son worked a summer job and made $9,000. On this $9,000 of wages, he had $100 of federal taxes withheld on his paychecks. He is not *required* to file a tax return since the $9,000 is considered earned income; and he is not above the standard deduction. But if he files a tax return, his tax liability will be zero and the government will send him his $100 refund.

I have talked to many parents about this, and sometimes they'll say, "That's great! But do I have to pay someone to prepare my kid's return?" If you need to pay $400 to a tax preparer to get $100 back in the form of a federal refund, then perhaps it's not worth it. But if you or your child can file it, the return certainly doesn't hurt.

My Kid Is in a Lower Tax Bracket . . . So Can I Give Them My Investments?

Most of the income taxes you pay are based on graduated tax rates. This simply means that the more money you make, the higher your tax rate. It's how our federal tax system works, and it's also how most state income taxes work. This generally means a child will pay a lower tax rate (because they have less income) than you will. Your kid might only pay a 10 percent federal tax rate on her income, while you pay 24 percent on yours.

Because your child likely has a lower tax rate, you might wonder if you can give some of your investments that generate interest, dividends, and capital gains to your child. You won't own them anymore, but they will still be in the family. And after all, isn't it better to give less money to Uncle Sam?

The problem is that the IRS has already figured out this strategy. In fact, they figured it out a long time ago. In response, they implemented something called the kiddie tax.

The kiddie tax works like this. If your child is a dependent and they generate too much investment income, the investment income gets taxed at the parent's tax rate (your tax rate)—rather than their own lower tax rate. If this happens, there are no real tax savings. The investment income is getting taxed the same way that it would if you had just held on to your investments!

The first $1,350 of investment income your child has is not taxable. The next $1,350 would be taxed at your child's tax rate.[53] Any investment income above this is taxed at your tax rate. An example may help:

Say your child is in the 10 percent tax bracket, while you are in the 24 percent tax bracket. Your child's only income is interest of $5,000. Her tax would basically be calculated as follows:

$1,350 x 0% = No taxes

$1,350 x 10% = $135 (her tax rate of 10 percent)

$2,300 x 24% = $552 (your tax rate of 24 percent)[54]

Total Taxes = $687

A few things to keep in mind before you tear up your promise to give your child your stock portfolio. First, remember the kiddie tax only applies when your child is a dependent. If they are above the age limits, out of college and working, or married, they may not be your dependent. If they are not your dependent, they pay taxes at their own rate—not yours.

Second, notice that a limited amount of investment income (the first $2,700 in 2025) is subject to no taxes or to your child's tax rate. Therefore, it may still be possible for you to give *some* assets to your child and still take advantage of the lower tax rates. They just can't exceed the kiddie tax threshold.

Third, the kiddie tax threshold does generally increase each year with inflation. It was $2,700 in 2025, but if history continues to repeat itself, it will increase each year. Also, the kiddie tax only applies when your tax rate is higher than your child's tax rate. If there is a minimal

---

53 These are 2025 numbers. So basically, any investment income above $2,700 is taxed at the parent's tax rate. This is the kiddie tax!

54 This is a greatly simplified example. The actual calculation of the kiddie tax may be more complicated due to graduated rates and the type of investment income being generated. However, the point here is that the kiddie tax may eliminate (or significantly reduce) the appeal of giving assets to kids.

difference between your tax rate and your child's tax rate, the kiddie tax may not matter too much.

Fourth, we should mention that there are limits on how much you can give to each of your children each year. In general, you can give up to $19,000 (in 2025) to each child in a given year and not have to pay gift taxes or file a gift tax return.

The Moral of the Story

Most of the tax incentives related to children are for working-class or lower-income parents. The phaseout of the child tax credit and the kiddie tax essentially minimizes tax savings for higher-income parents who have children. If you are a lower-income or working-class taxpayer, you can normally take advantage of the child tax credit, earned income credit, and many of the other incentives we mentioned.

Remember where we started, though. Everything is based on the idea of dependency. You have to figure out if you have a dependent first before you can see if any of these tax incentives matter for your situation!

Tips for Maximizing Savings: The Costs of a Kid

1. If you have kids in daycare or they stay with someone after school, make a list of your payments to the caretaker. Keep invoices as well. You may be able to take advantage of a dependent care credit. You will need your caretaker's tax ID or Social Security number to take the credit on your personal tax return.
2. The earned income tax credit (EIC) is one of the most commonly missed credits for lower-income families with children.

It is missed so often, the IRS actually has a form letter they send to people who they think may qualify. Be sure to check for this credit every year before filing your return! The earned income credit is one of the more lucrative tax credits. You could be leaving money on the table!

3. Kids get sick regularly—especially early in life. They pick up germs from the bus, other kids, and by just . . . well, being kids! Keep track of how much you pay for doctors, prescription drugs, eyeglasses, and other medical expenses for children. You may be surprised at how much you spend—and it might be worth a medical expense deduction, if it is a big enough expenditure!

CHAPTER 6

Airbnb and Rentals: What Hosts Can Deduct

There are a few things I think nearly everyone has tried or wants to try in life. Playing guitar or being the lead singer in a rock band comes to mind. Training for a marathon, climbing a mountain, or performing some other physical challenge is another. A third one might be owning rental property. Perhaps it's because many of us are still scarred from writing a rent check to a landlord, or it's just a vision of the American dream, but many people enjoy the idea of owning property (and receiving that rent check, rather than writing it).

Owning rental property is really just another form of investing. Like investing in stocks or bonds, when you put money into a house or condo, you want a return. You want it to either appreciate in value, produce income, or both. Just like any other market, the real estate market has ups and downs. However, over long periods of time, real estate values have normally increased, making it an understandably attractive prospect.

We should also point out that you can invest in real estate without buying a rental property. For example, you could invest in a real estate investment trust (REIT) or a real estate investment company (RIC).

These are funds made up of investments in multiple real estate properties. From my experience, though, many people choose not to go that route. Perhaps we feel more comfortable investing in assets we can see and touch, or maybe we feel like we know something about real estate (after all, we have all lived somewhere, right?). Whatever the reason, my experience has shown me there is a certain allure to buying real estate.

The steep price tag is perhaps the biggest deterrent that keeps many people from buying rental properties. Even cheap fixer-uppers are still more than many people are willing to pay to achieve their dream of owning real estate. However, Airbnb has made this less of an issue. While you can use Airbnb to rent out a property you've purchased, you don't have to. You can rent out your primary home if you want to! You can even just rent out one room or a backhouse. You can take an asset you already own and get some extra money to help pay the mortgage. Is this a great world or what?

If you *do* decide to take the plunge into the world of rental property, there are some great tax incentives out there. If you are a seasoned professional with rental property, there are plenty of ways you can reduce your income tax bill. The good news is, though—you don't have to be. Even if you are a novice, there are often some ways you can save a few bucks too. We will spend most of our time here dealing with the novices.

Does Passive Revenue Pull Its Weight?

The first thing we need to understand is the difference between passive and active revenue. Active income is generally income you need to put in time, energy, and effort to get, like wages or income from running your own business.[55] Passive income is income you generally get without putting in a proportionate number of hours or amount of energy.

Section 469(c)(2) of the Internal Revenue Code says all revenue from rental properties is considered passive. This shouldn't be surprising because you don't necessarily have to put in much effort to attract rental income. Your tenants normally have to pay rent even if you don't actually put in any time on the property. Contrast that with wages from your job, which is considered active income. You have to show up to your job every day and put in time, effort, and energy. While the tax laws are a bit more prescriptive in the determination of active versus passive income (and a bit more complex), it's pretty easy to see this distinction in broad strokes.[56]

Both active and passive income are taxable, and both types of income are taxed at the same rate. So why does the tax code make a distinction between active and passive income? It has to do with how losses from passive activities are treated. While losses from an activity you are active in (like a trade or business that you run forty hours per week) are normally deductible in full, passive losses are generally deductible in years where you have a net positive passive income.

It helps to illustrate this idea through an example. Let's say you collect $5,000 in one year's rent from a rental property. You also have deductions totaling $6,000 on your rental property. You get to deduct $1,000 in losses, right? Nope. Our tax code says that since you have a passive loss of $1,000, you can't deduct it this year. You have to wait until future years to take it against future income.

Let's continue on with the same example. Say the next year comes, and you collect the same $5,000 in rent. This year, you didn't have as

55 Technically, distributions from a retirement account (like an IRA or a 401(k)) are also considered active income. You worked for this money originally, so it is considered active income when you pull it out of a retirement account.

56 There are other types of income besides active and passive. For example, most investment income is considered portfolio income and is treated differently in certain contexts. That's beyond the scope of our discussion here though, so don't worry about that!

many repairs to make, so you only have $3,000 worth of deductions. Normally, you would show taxable income of $2,000 ($5,000 - $3,000). However, remember that passive loss you had last year? You can now take that loss against this income. So, you would show $1,000 in income ($5,000 income this year - $3,000 in expenses - $1,000 loss from last year) this year. On your tax return, you would show no income in the first year (and no losses) and $1,000 in income in the second year (the $2,000 of income from that year minus the $1,000 loss from the prior year). You wouldn't show a loss in either year.

Why is this important? Many people commonly set rent at a level that results in a loss each year. They figure they will reduce their taxes with the rental property by declaring losses, and then be able to sell the property for a large capital gain (which, as we discussed earlier, is taxed at a lower rate than ordinary taxes). As you can see, though, this strategy doesn't normally work. If your rental losses are all passive, you can't use any of them. You would declare no income on the tax return, but you would simply build up a larger and larger amount of passive losses each year. You would eventually be able to take these losses once you sell the property, but that might not be until several years later! Also, as we will see a bit later, the capital gain may not be as tax advantageous as many people think.

The point is that (with rare exceptions), buying rental property only with the intent of creating more tax deductions is not a good strategy.[57] Passive income and losses are treated differently. However, rental losses can be helpful to offset some of the other passive income you have on the return already. For example, let's say you have two rental properties. One is producing income, while the other is producing losses. The rental property that is producing losses can help reduce your income from the other rental property. Passive losses can offset

57 Real estate professionals are generally able to take their losses in full. They are not subject to the passive activity rules. If you work a full-time job in something non-real estate related (like an accountant or doctor), then you are unlikely to qualify as a real estate professional.

your income—but only to the extent that you have passive income. If that's the case, then having a rental property that produces losses can be a great way to save money on your tax return.[58]

Depreciation Sounds Bad. Is It?

When people hear the word depreciation, it often brings up connotations of things losing value. For example, people might associate depreciation with a car that comes off the lot and immediately loses value. However, in Tax Land, depreciation is actually a good thing. One of the biggest deductions many rental property owners take is depreciation.

Depreciation is an accounting method that spreads the cost of an asset over the span of time it is used for. For example, when you buy a property, you can't take a deduction for the entire cost of the property right away. Instead, depreciation is when you spread the deductions over a period of time. Depreciation is meant to approximate the normal wear and tear a rental property experiences. However, it does not go up over time, nor is it approximated. It is an amount that the IRS says you can take as a deduction each year. If you are renting out the property to individuals, you deduct your depreciation evenly (the same amount each year) over twenty-seven and a half years. If you are renting out the property to a business, you deduct your depreciation over thirty-nine years (again, the same amount each year).

Let's say that you buy a property for $275,000. You then rent it out to a family who has just moved to the neighborhood. You would be able to deduct $10,000 in depreciation each year:

$275,000 purchase price / 27.5 years = $10,000 of depreciation each year

---

58 To avoid issues with the IRS regarding the amount of rent you charge, it is always best to price rent in line with the market rate for a particular area. Check out available websites and reliable sources to determine how much should be charged by looking at comparable values for the area.

For the years you take a depreciation deduction, it may be possible for you to be cash-flow positive but actually pay no taxes related to the property on your tax return. Let's say that you collect rent during a year of $25,000 and you have other expenses (besides depreciation) of $15,000. You would have a positive cash flow of $10,000 ($25,000 - $15,000). However, if you had a $10,000 depreciation deduction, your net income from the rental property would be zero:

$25,000 rent collected - $15,000 expenses - $10,000 depreciation = $0 taxable income

This strategy can work well, especially if the property has relatively predictable expenses from one year to the next.

What Else Can You Deduct Besides Depreciation?

When we discussed side gigs, we talked about how any expense that's ordinary, necessary, and reasonable is deductible against income from a side gig. When it comes to rental property, the rules are very similar. In addition to depreciation, you can deduct items like small repairs, lawn care maintenance, HOA fees, real estate taxes, mortgage interest, house cleaning, pest control, and other maintenance and upkeep costs. Utilities, internet, phone, and television costs are deductible as well. Big expenditures (like constructing an addition or replacing a roof) cannot be deducted right away. These costs need to be taken over time using depreciation—similar to the cost of the property itself.

To alleviate the headaches of securing tenants and collecting rent, many owners will engage the services of a property manager. The fee property managers charge is deductible as well. Most of the normal costs of owning a home are deductible in full. Like our discussion on side gigs, the costs are deductible when you pay for them (cash basis).

It is possible to pay some costs in December (rather than January) to lower your tax bill in the current year.

What Is QBI? Do I Need to See a Doctor for It?

One other possibility is the Qualified Business Income (QBI) deduction available on the individual tax return. Using the QBI, you can take a deduction up to 20 percent of your net income from the property (rents collected minus deductions, including depreciation). To qualify for the QBI deduction, you normally have to meet all of the following requirements:[59]

- Maintain separate books and records to reflect income and expenses for each rental real estate property you own.
- Spend at least 250 hours during the year working on things related to the property.[60]
- Maintain time reports, logs, or similar documents, regarding the following: hours of all services performed; description of all services performed; dates on which such services were performed; and who performed the services.
- Attach a statement to the return stating you meet these requirements for the tax year you are taking the QBI deduction.

---

59 Rev. Proc. 2019-38. It is technically possible to qualify for the QBI deduction without meeting these requirements. This is actually just the requirements to meet the safe harbor rules.

60 This is a tricky requirement. Technically, it doesn't have to be *you* who actually does the work. For example, a maintenance worker you employ generally counts toward the hours requirement. There are certain situations in which contracted hours may count as well. The best move is to talk to a tax professional to be sure you are counting hours in the right way. You are welcome to reach out to me as well (davidpetersprofessionaleducation.com).

Lack of documentation keeps many rental property owners from taking this deduction. Even if you qualify, if you can't prove it, the IRS won't let you take it.

If you meet these requirements, you will be able to take a deduction on your personal income tax return. In general, the deduction may become something less than 20 percent of rental income if you have taxable income on your personal return in 2025 greater than:

- Married filing jointly: $394,600
- All others: $197,300

So, if you own rental property that you put some time into, but you are not a real estate mogul, this can be a helpful deduction. It is made to help people who don't spend all of their time in real estate activities, but they do have profitable rentals. If this describes you, this can seriously cut your tax bill. After all, there are very few deductions that are going to equal 20% of your net income from your rental!

Any More Special Deductions?

Remember that rental income is considered passive, which means your losses are not deductible right away. If you are a real estate professional, you might be able to deduct your losses. However, if you are just renting out a house on the side, it's hard to get around the passive loss rules.

There is one thing, though, that a non-real estate professional may be able to take advantage of: the deduction for active participation in a rental property. This is generally for people who have more moderate levels of income but just happen to own a rental property or two. If you meet the following requirements, you can deduct up to $25,000 in passive losses on your rental property:[61]

61 Sec. 469(i)

- Taxpayer must own at least a 10 percent interest in the activity; and
- Taxpayer must participate in management decisions in a bona fide sense. (Management decisions might include setting rents, reviewing tenant applications, repairing items on the property, and so on).

This can be a valuable deduction because it fits the case of many people. Even if you just own a rental property on the side, you could still take up to $25,000 in losses (a loss is when you have deductions, including depreciation, greater than the rent you collected).

In my experience, many clients are confused by this deduction. It seems to run counter to the logic we talked about earlier—you can only take passive activity losses to the extent you have passive activity income. This deduction is an exception to the passive activity loss rule. In other words, if you meet these requirements, you get to break the rules and take some losses on your return (up to $25,000). Again, this deduction exists to incentivize people with moderate levels of income to invest in rental properties.

The one difficulty about this particular deduction: It starts to phase out once you have an adjusted gross income on your tax return greater than $100,000. You are unable to take any deduction for losses on your rental property if you have an adjusted gross income of $150,000 or more. If you have enough money to afford to buy a rental property, it is very possible that your income is $150,000 or more. If that's the case, you don't meet this exception—and you can't deduct losses from your rental. In other words, we go back to the default rule: You can only take passive activity losses to the extent you have passive activity income.

However, if you don't make over $100,000 per year, this can be a sizable deduction! If your rental property happens to lose money in a given year, at least you get the advantage of taking a good chunk of that loss this year!

What If I Am Renting Out Only a Room or Two?

There are many ways people utilize Airbnb or similar sites. If you bought a separate home to rent out as an Airbnb, the IRS treats it like any other rental property, and the rules we have discussed here so far generally apply. However, what happens if you are renting out your own home? Similarly, what happens if you are only renting out a room or two within your house?

In either of these scenarios, you would generally need to allocate your deductions as personal or business. For example, say you rent out your home seventy-three days during the year. You use it the rest of the year as your personal residence. In this situation, you would generally need to allocate 20 percent of your expenses against your rental income:

73 days of rental use / 365 days = 20% rental usage

Rental income and expenses are shown on Schedule E of your personal tax return. You would show the amount of rent you collected for the year and then 20 percent of your expenses. You'd also show 20 percent of your mortgage interest, 20 percent of real estate taxes, 20 percent of your HOA fees, 20 percent of your utilities, and so on.

If you are just renting out a room or two, the logic is basically the same, except you need to consider the square footage of your rental area in comparison to the square footage of the entire house. For example, let's say you rent out a 500-square-foot room for seventy-three days (20 percent of the year). Your entire house comprises 2,000 square feet. This means you are renting out 25 percent of your house (500-square-foot room / 2,000-square-foot house) for 20 percent of the year (73 days / 365 days). Therefore, you would be able to take 5 percent of your expenses:

25% of the house x 20% of the year = 5% rental usage

A few things should be noted. First, the IRS considers any day that is not a day you rent out your house a personal use day. Second, any losses you have are generally not deductible if you are renting out your main home. The rules here are complex, so it's best to see a tax practitioner if you have a loss on your main home that you are renting out for part of the year.[62]

Third, remember the QBI deduction from earlier? You can't take a QBI deduction on the rental income generated from your personal residence.

Finally, remember that mortgage interest and real estate taxes are deductible as an itemized deduction on your personal tax return (on Schedule A). Therefore, the 80 percent personal use on mortgage interest and real estate taxes could still be deducted as a personal itemized deduction in most cases. It would just not be taken against your rental income on Schedule E. You can't take HOA fees, utilities, depreciation, or any of the other items we mentioned as a personal itemized deduction on Schedule A—only real estate taxes and mortgage interest. The 80 percent personal portion of these other expenses would not be deductible.

To many clients, this last part is confusing. If the entire amount of mortgage interest and real estate taxes is deductible, then does it really matter where I put it on the return? Why not put it all against rental income, for example, on Schedule E?

Where you put things on the return affects the overall calculation of the taxes you owe. You need to separate out expenses between rental (Schedule E) and personal (Schedule A), so your taxes are calculated correctly. Putting everything down as a personal or rental expense may result in a lower or higher tax liability. It also may cause you to receive a letter from the IRS! It's important to put things on the correct form. It's also important to keep the personal portion of non-deductible expenses off Schedule A. Never show HOA fees or any other non-deductible personal expense on Schedule A!

---

62 Sec. 280A

The Fifteen-Day Rule for Completely Tax-Free Income

This one is almost too good to be true. After all, it isn't often we get a good break from the Internal Revenue Code, right? Yet here it is: If you rent out your personal residence for less than fifteen days during the year, you don't have to declare any rental income. You heard me right. Go ahead and re-read the last sentence if you have to. It is not a misprint! If you rent out your personal residence for less than fifteen days during the tax year, you don't have to declare any of the rent you collect![63]

Professionals in the tax preparation game sometimes refer to this as the "Augusta Rule." For those of you who are golf enthusiasts, you probably know the Masters golf tournament takes place in Augusta, GA, each year. During that time, people who actually live in Augusta often rent out their homes for a few weeks to Masters spectators. Because people are traveling from long distances and housing is at a premium, golf enthusiasts are often willing to pay large amounts of money for a place to stay. As long as they are not in the Augusta homeowner's residence for more than two weeks, the rent collected does not have to be declared on their tax return. It doesn't matter how much they collect. It is all tax-free at the federal level!

Like seemingly everything in Tax Land, there *are* a few caveats. First, the less-than-fifteen-day rule only applies if you are renting out your primary residence. If you are renting out a secondary residence, it is considered a rental property, and the fifteen-day rule does not apply.

Second, the fifteen-day rule only applies at the federal level. In other words, you don't have to pay federal taxes on this income, but you may have to pay state or local taxes. This depends on the circumstances and where you reside. However, it is important to remember that some state tax laws are the same as federal tax laws, while others are different.

63 Sec. 280A(g)

However, this is a great strategy for someone who lives near a big yearly event—the Indy 500, The Masters, or any other regular event. You can get out of town, skip the traffic, make a few bucks on your home, and not pay a dime in federal taxes!

What If I Decide to Sell My Rental Property?

If you decide to sell your rental property, you generally need to declare any gain or loss you may have had on the sale. You'd take the amount of proceeds you receive from the sale minus your basis in the property. If your proceeds are greater than your basis, you have a gain. If your proceeds are less than your basis, you have a loss. It's not unusual for real estate to increase substantially in value over long periods of time (especially if situated in a growing area of the country). Therefore, in the year you sell your property, you may need to report a large gain on your tax return.

We should also point out that your basis is normally equal to the cost of the property (plus any improvements) minus depreciation. [64] Remember those depreciation deductions we mentioned earlier? They actually reduce your basis in the property—and increase the gain you need to declare when you sell.

Let's say you buy a rental home for $250,000. Over a period of five years, you deduct a total of $50,000 of depreciation. This year, you sell the property for $350,000. You would have a $150,000 gain that you must pay taxes on:

$250,000 purchase price - $50,000 depreciation = $200,000 basis

$350,000 sales price - $200,000 basis = $150,000 gain

---

64 The cost of the property includes amounts financed through a mortgage. For example, say you have a property that costs $500,000. You make a down payment of $100,000 and finance $400,000 of the cost through a mortgage. The cost of the property for tax purposes would be $500,000—not just the $100,000 you put in.

So, every year you take depreciation, you essentially make any gain you might need to declare higher. Unfortunately, it is not an option to just skip your depreciation deduction either. The IRS makes you calculate your gain when you sell as if you took the depreciation deductions each year (even if you forgot to take it). For example, let's say in the example we just did that you decided not to take any of the $50,000 of depreciation on your tax return. You were entitled to take these depreciation deductions, but you didn't do it. In this instance, your gain would still be $150,000—and you didn't even take your depreciation deductions![65]

The moral of the story: Always make sure you take the amount of depreciation deductions to which you are entitled each year. Don't skip them. It won't help. Take your deductions and lower your tax bill as much as you can as soon as you can!

When you sell your property, you may have to reimburse the IRS for the depreciation deductions you took earlier. However, taking deductions now can help you save some tax money before you sell.

Selling Rental Property Is a Capital Gain, so Don't I Get a Lower Tax Rate?

This is partially correct. It's actually a bit more complicated than that because a different capital gains rate is likely to apply on the sale of rental property. If you remember earlier on, we talked about two different types of capital gains—short-term and long-term. If you have owned the property for more than a year, you get the lower long-term

---

65 This is sometimes referred to as the allowed or allowable rule. The IRS assumes you took the amount of depreciation deductions you were allowed—whether you did or not!

capital gains rate. The long-term capital gains rate is normally 0 percent, 15 percent, or 20 percent at the federal level. If you were to sell property after owning it for a year or less, the gain would be a short-term capital gain and subject to the higher ordinary income tax rates.

But in most cases, this shouldn't be an issue. If you are planning on renting a place out, chances are good you will own the property for over a year (probably many years), so you'll generally be eligible for the lower long-term capital gains rates.

Unfortunately, though, the calculation complications don't end there. We have to account for another tax rate in addition to the long-term capital gains rate—the unrecaptured Section 1250 gains rate, which is equal to 25 percent. (We will just call it the 25 percent rate for our own sanity, okay?) The 25 percent rate applies to the extent we have depreciated the property. Once again, it is best to understand this idea through an example:

Let's say you bought a rental property several years ago for $250,000. You take the depreciation deduction over several years equal to $50,000. You then sell the property in the current year for $350,000. Your total gain would be $150,000:

$250,000 purchase price - $50,000 depreciation = $200,000 basis

$350,000 sales price - $200,000 basis = $150,000 gain

However, since you took $50,000 of depreciation deductions, the first $50,000 of gain would be taxed at a 25 percent rate. The next $100,000 of gains would be taxed at the long-term capital gains rate (either 0 percent, 15 percent, or 20 percent).

This is typically referred to as depreciation recapture by tax professionals. But the terminology is less important than the actual concept. The big thing to remember is that even if you hold a rental property for over a year and sell it, the entire gain will not be taxed at the more favorable long-term capital gains rates (0 percent, 15 percent, or 20 percent). Part of it will be subject to a 25 percent rate.[66] Plus, many states tax capital gains too. However, this is still a good deal, knowing the majority of the capital gains income will be taxed at the lower rate.

This Is a Lot!

The tax rules around rental properties are very detailed and can be difficult to navigate. This is not terribly surprising because people rent out property in many different ways. It really is impossible for us to consider all of the possibilities, even in a book like this. Just like anything else in Tax Land, if you get in over your head, it may be time to reach out to a tax attorney or a tax practitioner. They can help if your situation is too complicated to be addressed in this book.

Tips for Maximizing Savings: Rental Properties

1. Remember, any expenditure you make on the property is generally deductible (just like with a side gig). Be sure you get all your deductions. The easiest way to do this is to have a separate checking account for the rental property where you deposit the rent you collect and pay the bills. If everything is running through the same account, you will easily see your deductions at the end of the year.
2. Keep a log of the time you spend on your rental property. If you

66 The 25 percent rate is a maximum tax rate. That means it will never be more than your regular income tax rate. Let's say you have an ordinary tax rate of 22 percent. In that case, your 25 percent gain would not be taxed at a 25 percent rate—it would be taxed at 22 percent (your ordinary income tax rate).

can document you spend 250 hours or more on a rental property in a year, you can take advantage of the QBI deduction. It'll pay off to keep the log throughout the year and will prepare you for an audit. (And make your tax preparer happy because you are organized!)

3. Take all of the depreciation deductions you are entitled to on your rental property. It will slash dollars off your tax bill now and save you some headaches in the future when you sell the property.

CHAPTER 7

How to Save a Few Bucks in Retirement

"Look at that! No wages. How lazy am I?" My client smiled warmly. "Seriously, though, this feels very different to me. What should I be doing?"

"This is definitely a year of transition for you," I said, stating the obvious. "During the first year of retirement, we need to review your withholding. When you were working, you used to get nearly all of your withholding from your paycheck. Now that you are retired, you don't have a paycheck, so we need to look at where your tax payments will come from."

"Yeah, so am I going to pay less taxes now?" His brown eyes met mine. I could tell he was anxious, excited, happy, and nervous all at the same time. He wasn't much different from many other retiree clients. The year right after they retire is when they are adjusting to new ways of spending their time and freedom from work, but also a new sense of reliance on their money. For the first time ever, they are depending on their portfolio and retirement accounts to make sure they get by.

For most retirees, this means uncertainty. Every dollar counts, and they want to make sure they are being as tax-efficient as possible.

However, as I explained to my client in this situation (and many other clients before and since him), you actually have more control over your tax situation as a retiree than at any other point in your life.

You Say I Have More Control?

I learned a favorite saying from one of my first bosses at a CPA firm I worked for long ago: Wages are hard to move. What he meant is that there isn't much tax planning you can do around wages. You get paid to do your job, and you have to declare the income on the tax return. You can make 401(k) contributions and maybe even stick some money in an HSA (we talked about those things earlier), but the fact is, you really have to just take the wages on your tax return. When you are working, you can't do much except declare wages.

When you are retired, however, you don't have wages anymore. You are usually reliant on three sources of income: your portfolio, retirement accounts, and Social Security. On your portfolio, you won't have any capital gains until you sell something. You may need to declare interest and dividends, but only if you invest in stocks, bonds, or funds that generate this type of income. Your portfolio does produce taxable income, but you usually have a lot of control over the type, amount, and timing of that income.

When it comes to retirement accounts, you control the timing of the income as well. It is only when you make a distribution from a traditional retirement account that you need to declare income. While the IRS does make you pull a minimal amount out each year (called a Required Minimum Distribution or RMD), anything beyond that is really up to you. You need to pull what you need, but you can normally control how much.

Out of the three, Social Security may be the one you have the least control over. After all, the government just sends you a check. However, you don't need to take Social Security right away. In fact, if you want to, you can wait until age seventy to take Social Security. As an added bonus, your check will be considerably higher if you take it at age seventy![67] Even once you begin receiving a Social Security check, you may still be able to control some of the income that you have to declare. If you have low enough income, you don't have to declare any Social Security income on your federal tax return. The most that anyone gets taxed on is 85 percent of their Social Security income on their federal return. No one gets taxed on 100 percent of their Social Security benefits on their federal tax return. There are also several states that do not tax Social Security benefits.

As you can see, most retirees can control their taxable income better once they are no longer working. Wages are hard to move, but most of the sources of income for retirees are not. They can be deferred (put off until later tax years) or, in certain cases, even not declared on the tax return at all!

Does That Mean I Can Control My Tax Rate?

It sure does (within reason)! As I have told many clients, one of the most important aspects of tax planning when it comes to retirees is bracket management. Our federal tax system (and most state tax systems) is a graduated rate structure. In other words, the more taxable income you have, the higher the percentage of tax you pay. When you engage in bracket management, you are making sure you don't jump up to another higher tax bracket.

Say you are retired and need $5,000 to fund a trip to see your grandkids. You look at your tax return from last year and you realize you're in the 24 percent tax bracket. If you had had $2,000 more

---

67 If you were born after 1960, your check will be about 24 percent higher if you wait until age seventy to take Social Security (as opposed to taking it at age sixty-seven).

in income last year, you would have jumped up to the 32 percent tax bracket. You still managed to be in the 24 percent bracket last year—but barely. You decide it's probably best to pull money from one of your retirement accounts to fund your trip, since you don't have the money in checking or savings. You can pull the $5,000 from your traditional IRA, but that would be $5,000 of additional taxable income on your return this year. Not to mention, it would most likely put you into the 32 percent tax bracket. Another option is to pull the $5,000 from your Roth IRA. When you pull money from a Roth, it's tax-free because you've owned the account for many years. You decide to pull the money from the Roth so you don't jump a tax bracket.

This example of bracket management is important for all taxpayers, but especially for retirees—you have so much control over your tax return when you are retired. You want to make sure your tax return is predictable and that you essentially break even each year (no refund and no balance due).

Remember, the tax return is merely a reconciliation of the year that just passed. The perfect spot is if you have enough withholding or estimated tax payments to cover your tax liability, but nothing more. A big refund usually means you gave the government an interest-free loan for the entire year in the form of withholding or estimated tax payments. You don't want to give them too much. However, you also don't want to risk an underpayment penalty either. If you pay too little in withholding and estimated taxes, you'll get penalized. Therefore, you want to hit it right on the nose—no refund and no balance due (or as close to this as possible).

The only way the tax return becomes that predictable, though, is if you actively engage in bracket management. You need to make specific moves to reduce or lessen taxable income where possible throughout the year. Let's talk about how to do that for each of the forms of income that most retirees have: portfolio income, income from retirement accounts, and Social Security.

What Is Loss Harvesting? Do I Need to Start Farming?

You can put your overalls back in the closet—loss harvesting is not an agricultural technique. Rather, it is one way to lessen your taxable income from your portfolio. Before we define it, a few reminders: As we discussed above, you don't pay taxes on capital gains until you actually sell an investment. The investment may generate interest or dividend income, but no capital gains will occur until the sale date. Additionally, you only pay taxes on your *net* capital gains. In other words, you only pay taxes on your capital gains minus your capital losses. A capital loss occurs when you sell an investment for less than you bought it for.

In most years, you will have some investments that increase in value and some that decrease. Let's say you need cash from your portfolio. Instead of selling only investments that have appreciated in value and generating lots of capital gains, you could sell some that have increased in value and some that have decreased at the same time. Either way, you will be able to generate the cash that you need. However, if you sell some winners (those investments that have increased in value) and some losers (those investments that have decreased), your net capital gains will be much lower. This is called loss harvesting.

Let's put some numbers to the concept. Say that you have a capital gain on ABC stock of $150. However, you bought your DEF stock for $200 and sold it in the same year for only $100. You would have a capital loss on your DEF stock sale of $100 ($200 - $100 = $100). In this instance, you would only be taxed on your net capital gains of $50 ($150 capital gain on ABC - $100 capital loss on DEF = $50 net capital gain).[68] Therefore, one way to keep your taxes down is to sell

68 Please note that we are greatly simplifying the netting process for capital gains. There is a little bit more to it than this, but in general, this is how it works. The major point here is that one way to avoid taxes is to generate capital gains and capital losses in the same year!

some investments that are winners in the same year you sell some that are losers.

It may not always be possible to have net capital gains of zero, but you can certainly reduce your taxes by generating some capital losses in the same year you have capital gains—a very simple but effective strategy![69]

Does It Matter Which Retirement Account I Pull From?

As we mentioned earlier, there are two basic types of retirement accounts: Roth and traditional. Contributions to a traditional IRA are typically deductible, unlike a Roth account. The Roth also has income limitations and may not be offered by certain employers.

In either case, if we leave the money in a Roth or a traditional retirement account, the money will grow tax-free. Any capital gains, interest, or dividends generated by the investments will not be taxable. Assuming the markets cooperate, your money will continue to grow inside the account until you are ready to withdraw in retirement. And in either case, if you withdraw the money prior to reaching age fifty-nine and a half, you will be subject to a tax penalty—even if you have decided you are retired at that point![70]

So what's the difference in withdrawing between the two? Any money you withdraw from a Roth account is generally going to be tax-free.

---

69 If you have more capital losses than capital gains in a year, then you have a net capital loss. You can normally deduct up to $3,000 of your capital losses in a given year ($1,500 if you file married filing separately). If you have capital losses above this amount, you are not able to deduct them in the current year. You will have to wait until a later year to deduct them if possible. This is referred to as a capital loss carryforward.

70 You also generally need to leave money in a Roth account for at least five years in order to avoid a tax penalty.

With Roth accounts, you don't get a tax deduction on the front end, but you also don't get taxed on the amount of the withdrawal either.

On the other hand, any money you withdraw from a traditional retirement account is taxable as ordinary income. Therefore, with a traditional account, you get the advantage of potentially tax-deductible contributions. However, you also have to pay taxes on the amounts you withdraw in retirement.

In my experience, I've never had a client get upset with me over having more tax-free income in retirement. Therefore, in general, I typically recommend that clients have at least some money in Roth retirement accounts if at all possible. This allows you to have some money available for withdrawal tax-free in retirement and can help keep you in a lower tax bracket. They will pay more in taxes now, but they can enjoy more tax-free income in the future!

How to Make the Most of Your Standard Deduction in Retirement

Whenever I tell clients this, they then assume it's best for them to pull *all* of their money out of any Roth accounts first. This will result in no taxable income. However, emptying your Roth account(s) exclusively before touching your traditional IRA is not necessarily a good strategy for a few reasons. First, the IRS makes you take out at least a minimum amount from your traditional retirement accounts each year, normally starting at age seventy-three. This is referred to as a required minimum distribution (RMD). So, if you are seventy-three or older and you take money only from Roth accounts, the IRS will penalize you.

Second, even if it were possible to only pull money from Roth accounts, it may simply defer the problem to any traditional retirement accounts you have. For example, say you have money in both traditional and Roth retirement accounts. In both, the money is growing tax-free. You decide to pull only from your Roth accounts. Assuming there are no issues with RMDs, your traditional retirement account funds continue to grow, and at some point, you need to pull the money out. The balance would continue to grow and grow, resulting in more and more taxable income in later years.

Third, you don't want to waste your standard deduction either. Let's say your standard deduction is $15,000. If you pull all money from your Roth retirement account, you will have no income to report—but you will also be wasting your standard deduction. Instead, you could pull $15,000 from your traditional retirement account and any remaining money from your Roth. If you do this, you'd report $15,000 in gross income on your tax return but then take a standard deduction of $15,000 as well. Your resulting taxable income would still be zero. You would still pay no taxes.

Why is this a better result? By at least pulling an amount equal to the standard deduction amount from a traditional account, you lessen the amount of funds that need to be withdrawn from your traditional accounts in later years. You have no taxes to pay either way, but the second option ensures your taxes in future years will be less, too. Your future you thanks your present you!

What Is an Annuity, and Do I Need One?

An annuity is a financial product often used to supplement someone's retirement income. There are various forms of annuities, but in all cases, you pay a sum of money (either through installments or a lump sum) to a financial institution (normally an insurance company), which then agrees to send you a series of payments over time.

The payments generally continue until the recipient passes away.[71] In this way, they provide a stable amount of income to someone who is retired. Instead of worrying about market fluctuations and the value of the portfolio dropping, recipients can have some peace of mind in knowing they'll have a certain amount of income each month for as long as they live. You can invest in an annuity inside a retirement account or outside of it.

From a tax perspective, any annuity income you receive is taxable. Whenever you receive a payment from an annuity, you are generally receiving two things. Part of the payment is simply paying back the money you invested in the annuity. The other part is income. It is the money the insurance company has made on your behalf while they've held the annuity. You pay taxes on the income portion, but not the basis portion (the return of the money you paid in).

While the thought of stable, consistent payments is comforting to many retirees, we should note that administrative fees on annuities can be expensive. If you can stand the volatility in the portfolio, you may be able to save some money on fees by simply pulling a regular amount of income from your retirement portfolio each year. This "self-made annuity" essentially saves you the administrative fees of an actual annuity, while also providing you with a consistent amount of cash flow each month—as long as you can stand the ups and downs of the markets!

RMDs, QCDs, and Other Acronym Soup

One thing we mentioned above was the concept of RMDs. As a reminder, that's a required minimum distribution, or the minimum

71 There are certain annuities that provide a guaranteed number of payments. If the person passes away before this minimum number of payments is reached, then the remaining payments are paid to the estate or a beneficiary. There is typically an additional cost for this guarantee though!

amount one is required to withdraw from an account. For most of your retirement accounts, you are required to begin taking at least a minimum amount out each year. RMDs for traditional IRAs (including SEPs and SIMPLEs) generally start at age seventy-three for most people. For Roth IRAs, there is no requirement to take any amount out while you are still living. As long as you are alive, you can withdraw the money or keep it in the account for as long as you like!

For those still working, many taxpayers don't have to begin RMDs either. For example, say you are still working at age seventy-three. You enjoy your job, so why quit? You have a 401(k) with your employer and a traditional IRA at the local bank you opened yourself. While you would need to take an RMD from your traditional IRA each year (because you are seventy-three in this example), you would not need to take anything from your employer 401(k) because you are still working.[72]

Note two things about this "still working" exception. It doesn't apply if you are still working and own the company. The tax law says that if you own 5 percent of the company or more, then you can't defer your RMDs. In other words, you would generally need to begin taking your RMDs at age seventy-three. Second, the exception only applies to your current employer's plan—not to any 401(k)s you might have through a previous employer.

Say you have a 401(k) plan with ABC Company, who you are currently working for. You also have an old 401(k) plan with DEF company. You never rolled over your DEF 401(k), so the funds are still in your old employer's (DEF) plan. You would need to begin taking RMDs from your 401(k) at DEF starting at age seventy-three because you are no longer working there. You would *not* need to begin taking RMDs from your ABC 401(k) plan since you are *currently* working

72 One thing to note is that this does not apply to SEPs and SIMPLEs. If you have a SEP or a SIMPLE through your employer, you generally need to begin taking RMDs at age seventy-three.

there. You can only defer taking RMDs from your current employer plan, not previous employers'.[73]

For some people, RMDs are more of a nuisance than anything. If you already have enough money through Social Security and your portfolio, you may not really need the RMD. In other words, you may just need to pull from your retirement account because the IRS says you have to. The RMD increases your taxable income. That's about it.

One way to avoid having to report taxable income from the RMD in this situation is to do a Qualified Charitable Distribution (QCD). A QCD is a direct transfer from your IRA to a charity. By doing a QCD, you can avoid reporting up to $100,000 in income on your tax return from your RMD. A QCD may be done with an IRA only—but it can reduce your tax liability substantially and help you support a cause you care about. Here is how it works.

Let's say you make enough money through Social Security and portfolio income to support yourself. You really love helping kids, though, and St. Jude Children's Hospital is one of your favorite places to donate money. You talk to your CPA, and she tells you to take an RMD from your IRA of $25,000 this year to avoid an IRS penalty. You can arrange for your custodian (such as Schwab, Fidelity, or Merrill Lynch) to send $25,000 directly to St. Jude as a QCD. This allows you to meet your RMD requirements with the IRS. No penalty. Also, the $25,000 would not be included in your taxable income this year, so you pay less in taxes as well.[74] Not to mention, you can feel good about

---

73 You could avoid this situation by simply rolling your old 401(k) into your current employer's plan, assuming the current plan takes rollovers. However, you can only do this before you need to start taking RMDs. Let's say you need to start taking RMDs at age seventy-three. You could roll your old 401(k) into your current employer plan during the year you turn seventy-two. No problem. But in the year you turn seventy-three, you would be stuck. You would have to take an RMD from the old plan. It is too late to do a rollover to avoid the RMD once you reach the year in which you need to begin taking RMDs!

74 If you do a QCD, you cannot also take a charitable contribution deduction. That would be double-dipping, so the IRS does not allow that. You can take one or the other—a QCD or a charitable deduction.

supporting a cause you champion. That's a win-win-win! Again, you can do a QCD up to $100,000, but it needs to be from an IRA. You can't do it with a 401(k) or any other type of retirement plan. If you don't need the money, though, this is a great way to cut your tax bill down in a meaningful way.

What About My Social Security Checks?

Most retirees are also entitled to Social Security benefits once they retire. Your Social Security retirement benefit is based on the highest thirty-five years of earnings while you're working. The Social Security Administration (SSA) takes your average monthly earnings from these thirty-five years and uses a formula to derive how much your monthly benefit will be.[75] This benefit is then adjusted up or down depending on when you take benefits. You can take benefits as early as age sixty-two. However, the SSA will reduce your monthly payment if you decide to take benefits before your full retirement age (FRA). If you are reading this book and you were born in 1960 or later, your full retirement age is sixty-seven. If you were born before that, your FRA is different. Conversely, you can wait to take Social Security until you reach age seventy. If you wait to pull benefits until after your full retirement age, you receive a larger payment.

There are lots of studies out there about the best time to pull Social Security benefits. While this can make for interesting reading (especially if you love mathematics), the advice is normally not very practical. None of us knows when we are going to die. Therefore, it is impossible to know how many Social Security payments we'll be entitled to in our lifetime. Unless we know how many payments we're going to

---

75 You generally need to work at least ten years (forty quarters) in order to receive Social Security retirement benefits.

get, it's impossible to know the perfect time to begin taking payments.

In my opinion, it's best to keep the problem simple. Wait on taking Social Security benefits as long as you can if you don't need the money. If you can get by on other sources of income, you will get a nice "bonus" (additional payment) at age seventy. If you need to pull sooner, that's fine. However, try to wait until your full retirement age so you don't get a reduced amount. You worked for the benefit, so why give some of it back to the government?

The good news is that no matter when you decide to claim benefits, Social Security is never 100 percent taxable. Depending on your other income sources, you may include 85 percent of Social Security benefits on your personal return, 50 percent of your benefits, or none. You only pay taxes on this percentage. As we mentioned earlier, this is how it works on your federal return only. Many states do not tax Social Security benefits.

The percentage of benefits you must include on your personal tax return is based on the following formula:

Modified Adjusted Gross Income + 50% of Social Security benefits + tax-exempt interest

The result of this formula is your provisional income. You then figure out how much of your Social Security benefits are taxable by plugging your provisional income into the following table:

<Social Security Provisional Income Table for 2025>

While the details of the calculation itself are difficult to master, the broad-stroke concepts are relatively easy. Modified Adjusted Gross Income (MAGI) encompasses all your normal items of income on your return, including wages, capital gains, dividends, interest, and income from retirement plan withdrawals. The higher your income from these items, the greater the percentage of your Social Security benefits that will be taxable.

The moral of the story is that you want to avoid one-time big hits on your taxable income when you are retired. If you have a large amount of income on your return in a given year, it will also make more of your Social Security income taxable. My grandmother would call this a double whammy!

For instance, say you are retired and want to buy a second home. You sell some investments to afford the down payment, resulting in a large amount of long-term capital gains. This increases your provisional income for Social Security benefit purposes. In some cases, it might move you from only having half (50 percent) of your Social Security benefits taxable to 85 percent. The total impact on your tax return could be much higher than the long-term capital gains!

At this point, go back to what we mentioned earlier about bracket management. Large one-time hits on the return, like large capital gains, big distributions from traditional retirement accounts, and bonuses from part-time work, can have a "snowball" effect on your return. They can bump you into another tax bracket and increase the percentage of taxable Social Security benefits. The best move is to keep a spreadsheet throughout the year to estimate your tax liability. That way, you can easily see the impact any one-time hits can have!

Can I Work While Receiving Social Security?

Sometimes people prefer to continue working either full-time or part-time, even after claiming Social Security benefits. The problem, though, is that your benefit payment is reduced even further if you work and claim Social Security before your full retirement age. The moral of the story is you shouldn't claim Social Security before you are done working. If you are still working, waiting to claim benefits is usually best. If you are still working at the full retirement age, this no longer matters. Once you reach the FRA, you can work as much as you want without it having any effect on your benefits!

What If I Have Not Worked, but My Spouse Did?

When it comes to Social Security, you'll typically receive **whichever is higher**: **your own benefit** (based on your highest thirty-five years of earnings) **or up to 50 percent of your spouse's benefit.** For example, if I had earned a Social Security benefit based on my own work of $4,000 per month and my spouse had earned a benefit based on their work of $5,000 per month, I would claim Social Security based on my own record—the $4,000 per month would be higher than 50 percent of my spouse's benefit. However, if my spouse had a benefit of $9,000 per month, 50 percent of their benefit would be $4,500—which would be higher than my own benefit of $4,000. So, I would choose to take the benefit based on 50 percent of my spouse's record.

It's not unusual for people to take some time away from the workforce. In my own family, my mother had a successful career as a nurse. She took some time away to raise my siblings and me when we were young. Once we got old enough, she started working again as a schoolteacher. In this instance, my mother would be able to claim benefits based on her own working record or 50 percent of my dad's benefit.

Even if you have been out of the workforce for a period of time, you should take a look at your Social Security benefits. You can always look at your projected benefit by logging into the Social Security Administration's website (www.ssa.gov). More than one of my clients has been surprised at how much they are entitled to!

Will Social Security Be There When I Retire?

Social Security is the federal safety net for retirees, those with disabilities, and survivors of workers who paid into it. The Social Security Act was originally signed in 1935 to provide Americans with some economic stability on the heels of the Great Depression, and it has supported many Americans in financially vulnerable positions ever since.

At the time of this writing, your Social Security benefit is calculated based on an inflation-adjusted average of your top thirty-five years of earnings.[76] This average benefit is then placed into a formula, which is then adjusted up or down depending on when you claim benefits. You can claim Social Security benefits as early as age sixty-two. However, if you do, you will receive a lower benefit than if you wait to claim. You can claim as late as age seventy, and this will increase your benefit as much as possible.[77]

For several years, media and financial advisors alike have debated whether Social Security has a future for retiring Americans. It's a valid concern. Taking away Social Security could be devastating to many Americans. If a retiree is highly dependent on their Social Security check and this benefit is pulled or shrunk, they could live in poverty with few prospects for employment. After all, if you are retired and receiving Social Security, health or age may limit your job prospects. Taking away Social Security without a comparable replacement would create complications, to say the least.

The concern is also valid considering how much has changed since Social Security was first enacted. The amount of time people spend in retirement has vastly increased over time due to seniors living longer and advances in medical technology. These days, it is not unusual to have someone spend twenty, thirty, or even forty years in retirement! This means longer payment streams from Social Security—and more strain on the system.

---

76 You are only credited with the amount of Social Security wages you earn up to the wage base for a particular year.

77 In general, you also must work at least ten years to be eligible for the full amount of Social Security retirement benefits.

Yet while many are quick to recite statistics around how quickly Social Security funds will run out, the system itself has been surprisingly resilient. Recent funding shortages have been rectified by simply raising the Social Security wage base. Employee wages are generally subject to the 6.2 percent FICA tax. However, the tax is no longer assessed once an employee reaches a higher-income level. One way to deal with the funding shortages in the system is to simply make it so that higher and higher wage levels are subject to the tax. This has been the solution opted for in more recent years, as opposed to raising the percentage of the tax or decreasing payouts. In a way, Social Security is the best annuity around, since it is backed by the US government and continues to make payments as long as you live—assuming it stays resilient.

Despite the relative resilience of the system, we can never be certain of the future. If you're nervous about the future of Social Security, the best thing to do may be to simply assume it will not be there when you retire. In other words, rely on other sources of funds in retirement, like company retirement plans, IRAs, and savings. That way, if it does end up being available, it will increase your total retirement benefits available. If it's not there, you were not depending on it anyway. In either case, you should have other benefits outside of Social Security.

Tips for Maximizing Savings: When You Are Retired

1. For retirees, bracket management is incredibly important. You have more control over the tax return than at any other point in your life. Try to get to a point where you break even on the return. No big refunds or balances due. Avoid jumping tax brackets by minimizing your taxable income.

2. Before pulling money from a brokerage account, consider selling some investments that have appreciated and some that have depreciated. Loss harvesting can reduce your tax liability and, in certain cases, allow you to pull from your portfolio tax-free!
3. Try to avoid one-time big hits on the tax return. If you know you will have a big capital gain on your return, see if you can reduce or eliminate it with an offsetting capital loss. You may also be able to offset income with a business loss.
4. Part-time employment before your full retirement age (age sixty-seven, if you were born after 1960) can reduce your Social Security benefit payment. It is best to hold off on claiming Social Security until you are certain you no longer want to be employed.

CHAPTER 8

Your Most Common Tax Questions, Answered

As a tax practitioner, I am constantly fielding questions from clients. We have touched on many of these in this book already: *Are my prescriptions deductible? Can I take a deduction when I donate my car to charity? What credits can I take advantage of now that my kid is in school? What happens when I pull money out in retirement?* However, even though we have covered a lot of ground in Tax Land, we have not addressed all of the most common questions. In this chapter, we are going to focus on some of the more common ones I see that we haven't addressed so far.

I just sold my old house and am buying a new one. Are there any tax incentives available?

Few expenditures in most people's lifetimes are bigger than buying a new house. Therefore, it is important to be prepared for it. If you can, you should try to put at least 20 percent down on the price. While it may be possible to put down a lower payment, you will normally have to pay the cost of private mortgage insurance (PMI) in addition to the cost of the mortgage itself. If you can't quite make the full 20 percent, put as much down as you can. The closer you are to 20 percent, the less the PMI premiums will be.

When looking for a mortgage, search for the lowest interest rate possible. This generally involves shopping around. To streamline the process, you can work with a mortgage loan originator (MLO). An MLO can shop your mortgage to various lenders to help you find the lowest rate. While they do take a fee for this service, it can be the most efficient way to find the lowest rate.

Owning your own home has various tax advantages as well. You can generally deduct any real estate taxes you pay (including any you may be responsible for in the year you buy). You can also deduct any mortgage interest as well, within certain limits. Many people combine the cost of their real estate taxes and mortgage into one payment. This does not affect their deductibility. Real estate taxes are still deductible, even if you include them in your mortgage payment. Both are itemized deductions on Schedule A.

If you need to sell your existing home, some tax incentives may help. First, you are still allowed to deduct any real estate taxes or mortgage interest you paid for the portion of the year you owned the home. If you lived and used your home as a primary residence (not a vacation home) for at least two years before you sell, you will be able to exclude the first $250,000 (if you are single) or $500,000 (if you are married) of capital gains from the sale. As a reminder, a capital gain occurs when you sell something for more than you bought it. If you are single and you sell your home for $350,000 after buying it for $50,000, you will have a capital gain of $300,000 ($350,000 - $50,000 = $300,000). Assuming you meet the two-year rule, you will only be taxed on $50,000 of this gain. The first $250,000 will be excluded from taxable income (due to Section 121). In other words, you won't pay taxes on the first $250,000 (or $500,000 if you are married). Because of this rule, most people can sell their home at a gain and not pay a dime in taxes!

Do I Need to Pay Estimated Taxes?

Our federal tax system (and state income tax systems) are pay-as-you-go. In other words, you don't pay taxes once per year—you pay them throughout the year. If you work for an employer, you pay taxes through withholding. Every single paycheck has an amount withheld for federal (and state) income taxes. In this way, the tax return is a reconciliation. You are reconciling what you owe versus how much you have paid during the year. If you have paid in more than you owe, you are entitled to a tax refund. If you owe more than you paid in, you have a balance due. April 15 is a time to square up with the taxing authorities.

In some situations, you may not have withholding taken from your check. The most common example is if you are self-employed. Unless you are paying yourself a salary and withholding taxes, most small business owners do not have any withholding. As another example, some retirees who are living primarily off their investment portfolio may not have any withholding. In these situations, the taxpayer will often need to make estimated tax payments (also known as quarterly tax payments) to the IRS (and any state authorities). They will do this by either sending in a check or paying electronically through the appropriate website. Estimated taxes are exactly what they sound like. It is an estimate of what you think you will owe on your tax return at the end of the year.

If you do not make estimated tax payments or have withholding taken out, the IRS has a system that penalizes people for not paying enough in taxes throughout the year. More specifically, if you don't pay enough either through withholding or estimated taxes or both, you need to pay a penalty in addition to the normal taxes you owe.

On your federal tax return, the amount you need to pay in through withholding and estimated taxes is based on your prior year and current year tax liabilities. If your federal tax liability in the current year is estimated to be less than $1,000, you do not need to make any estimated tax payments. You can simply square up on your tax return.

If you have AGI on your federal tax return in the prior year of $150,000 or less, you need to pay the US Treasury (through estimated taxes, withholding, or both) whichever is less:

- 100 percent of your prior year tax liability or
- 90 percent of your current year tax liability.

If you have AGI on your federal tax return in the prior year of more than $150,000, you need to pay (through withholding, estimated taxes, or both) whichever is less:

- 110 percent of your prior year tax liability or
- 90 percent of your current year tax liability.

You must still file a tax return, and you may still have a balance due even if you meet these thresholds. Meeting these thresholds helps you to avoid an underpayment penalty—it doesn't mean you won't pay taxes. An example may help.

Let's assume your AGI on your federal tax return last year was $93,000, and you had a federal tax liability equal to $12,000. This year, you anticipate your federal tax liability will be about $15,000, but you have already withheld $5,000 (this would be shown on your pay stub). How much would you need to pay in to avoid an underpayment penalty?

Since you were under $150,000 in AGI ($93,000), you would need to pay in the lesser of 100 percent of your prior year liability or 90 percent of your current year liability:

100 percent of last year = $12,000

90 percent of the current year = $15,000 x 90% = $13,500

In total, you would need to pay in at least $12,000 through either withholding or estimated tax payments this year to avoid an underpayment penalty (since 100 percent of last year is less). You already have withholding this year of $5,000, so you would need to pay in at least $7,000 more through either withholding or estimated tax payments ($12,000 - $5,000 = $7,000 more).

Let's say you decide to make a $7,000 estimated tax payment. That takes your total for estimated tax payments and withholding up to $12,000 for the current year. Does that mean you won't owe anything on your tax return? No, you will still owe something. If your tax liability turns out to be $15,000 for this year (like you estimated above), you have only paid in $12,000. You will still owe $3,000 ($15,000 tax liability - $12,000 in withholding and estimated tax payments = $3,000 balance due).

Let's take a step back from the details. You are never forced to make estimated tax payments. However, if you don't make them, the IRS will charge you a penalty. The more you miss the mark, the bigger the penalty. For example, if I am under the threshold by $10,000, I will pay a higher underpayment penalty than if I am under the threshold by $2,000. The worse you miss, the worse the penalty is.

Federal estimated tax payments for individuals are due on the following dates:

- 1st quarter: April 15
- 2nd quarter: June 15
- 3rd quarter: September 15
- 4th quarter: January 15

In general, you want to pay in one-fourth of your estimated tax payments each quarter. Also, there is no such thing as a late estimated tax payment. If you miss the due date, the payment will be applied to the next quarter. For example, let's say you miss the June 15 deadline for your Q2 estimated tax payment. You pay it on July 1. This payment would generally be applied to Q3.

If you live or work in a state with income tax, you may need to make estimated tax payments to it as well. In many cases, the rules and due dates for state income tax payments are similar to the federal system—but they may not be the same. For example, in my home state of Virginia, the Q1 estimated tax payment is actually due May 1.

If you have substantial income from sources without withholding, like investment income, Social Security income, or self-employment income, you may need to make estimated tax payments or increase your withholding.[78] You can increase your withholding by filling out a new Form W-4 and giving it to your employer (not the IRS). Or alternatively, you can make estimated tax payments directly on the IRS website or by mailing a check. Either way, it will save you some headaches in the long run and a potential big tax bill at the end of the year!

How Can I Lower the Tax Bill on My Investments?

When you are saving and investing, there are essentially three different kinds of taxable income you may encounter.

Interest Income

Interest income is the money that you receive for holding money in an interest-bearing account. You will receive interest income if you put your money in certificates of deposit, money market accounts, and savings accounts. Interest income is subject to normal taxes (ordinary income tax rates). You are taxed on interest income regardless of whether or not you transfer the money. For example, let's say you earn

78 Unless your employer has limitations, you can normally fill out a new W-4 anytime you like. The IRS has no limits on how often you fill out a W-4.

interest on a savings account. You may transfer that money to your checking account, keep it in savings, or perhaps withdraw it in cash. In any instance, you will still pay taxes on this amount.

Dividend Income

If you invest in stocks, the companies in which you invest may pay part of their profits out to you. This type of payment is referred to as a dividend. Dividends are subject to either regular taxes (ordinary income tax rates) or the lower long-term capital gains tax rates (more on this below). Sometimes people choose to reinvest dividends in the stock from which they came. For example, you might receive a dividend from ABC Company, but then use that dividend to simply buy more stock in ABC Company. Even reinvested dividends are subject to taxes. Like interest income, it does not matter if you transfer the dividend income out of your account or not. Either way, you must pay taxes on it.

Capital Gains

A capital gain is the difference between how much you sold an investment for and how much you paid. For example, if I bought a stock for $100 and sold it for $250, my capital gain would be $150 ($250 - $100 = $150). Capital gains are always taxable. However, the *rate* at which they are taxed will differ depending on how long you have held the investment. If you buy an investment and sell it one year or less from the date you bought it, the capital gain is subject to normal taxes (ordinary tax rates). If you buy an investment and sell it more than a year after you bought it, it is subject to a lower tax rate (the long-term capital gains rate). However, you pay a lower rate of tax if you hold the investment for more than a year.

In general, you want to try to keep the taxes you pay on investment income to a minimum. There are several simple strategies you can use:

Strategy 1: Loss Harvesting

We talked about loss harvesting in the chapter for retirees. You don't have to be a retiree to use loss harvesting as a strategy. It really just involves selling some appreciated and some depreciated investments anytime you need money. This is a great way to cut down your net capital gains—which means a lower tax bill overall!

Strategy 2: Tax-Efficient Investments

Certain types of investments are less likely to generate taxable income. For example, some companies do not regularly pay dividends. If you invest in them, you will not likely have dividend income. (You would only have capital gains income when you sell the investment.) Certain types of funds (exchange-traded funds and mutual funds) may specialize in investing in these types of companies (often referred to as growth funds). One way to save taxes is to simply invest money in these types of companies or funds.

Similarly, certain types of interest income are not taxable. Municipal bond interest is not subject to federal income taxes. (It may or may not be subject to state income taxes.) One way to save on taxes is to simply invest funds that will not generate taxable income.

But as my grandmother would say, you need to make sure the tail is not wagging the dog. Let's say you are retired and need your portfolio to generate dividends to provide cash flow for living expenses. If this is the case, investing in companies that don't pay a dividend doesn't make sense. You won't get the cash flow you need in order to live. While saving taxes is nice, you should make sure it fits with your overall portfolio strategy and financial goals. If you are not sure if this works, then consult an investment professional. That's what they are there for!

Strategy 3: Tax Location

Certain types of accounts allow money to grow tax-free. For example, if you put money into most retirement accounts (qualified plans or IRAs), any interest, dividends, and capital gains generated while the money is in the account are not taxed. As we stated earlier, long-term capital gains are taxed at a lower tax rate than interest and some dividend income. For this reason, one strategy is to invest in companies or funds that generate dividends and interest in your retirement accounts. Invest in companies or funds that are unlikely to generate these types of income in your regular (taxable) brokerage accounts.

Let's say I want to invest in bonds that will generate interest income. Assuming they are a permissible investment for the account type I have, I could potentially invest in the bonds through my 401(k). Since a 401(k) is a retirement account, the bonds will generate interest that is not taxable. Let's say I also want to invest in a growth stock fund that is unlikely to generate significant interest or dividend income. I could use my brokerage account to invest in the growth stock fund. That way, I would only pay taxes when I actually sold my ownership in the stock fund (capital gains).

Again, though, it is important to make sure that tax location strategies make sense for your overall financial goals. For example, the strategy we just described might ultimately lead to a lower stock allocation in your retirement account. This may not be ideal if you are not planning to retire for several years.

I just gave some money to a GoFundMe. Can I deduct that?

I truly believe there are a lot of good people in the world. I think back on my own life, and I am amazed at the level of kindness I have been shown by complete strangers or people who didn't owe me anything.

For this reason, I am not surprised at the popularity of crowdfunding websites. When people are passionate about a cause, they can give a small donation over the internet. While the lack of regulation and potential for deception when posting on crowdfunding websites is an ongoing concern, it is not unusual to see people giving to those who need help. The obvious question come tax time is: Can you deduct crowdfunding donations?

Unfortunately, most of the time, the answer is no. The reason for this is a distinction the IRS makes between charitable donations and gifts. Charitable donations are deductible, while gifts are not. To be considered a charitable donation, a payment needs to be made to an organization registered with the IRS as a charity.[79] Charities are not for the benefit of one individual. Think about it. Does Junior Achievement support financial education for one individual or the public? Does the SPCA support animal welfare for one pet in the community or as many pets as it can? Charities are organized to help the public at large. If you are helping one person, it is generally a gift. If you are giving a donation to a public charity or private foundation registered with the IRS that benefits multiple people, it's a charitable contribution.[80] Charitable contributions are deductible.

If you give more than $19,000 in 2025 to any individual, you will normally have to file a gift tax return. If you give gifts over your lifetime more than a certain amount ($15 million in 2025), you may have to pay gift taxes. That's right! Gift taxes are owed by the giver of the gifts, not the recipient!

If you receive payments from a crowdfunding website, it is generally not taxable income either—unless you are offering something

---

79 It is possible to take a charitable contribution deduction for contributions made to a private foundation or a public charity. The real issue is whether or not the organization has registered with the IRS.

80 The main difference between a public charity and a private foundation often comes down to who can make a donation. If donations are accepted by the public, it is a public charity. If donations are only made by one individual or a family, it is normally a private foundation.

in return for people's generosity. For example, if I am offering to give people limited edition collector's coffee mugs in exchange for their contribution to my GoFundMe, then this is business income (and it is taxable). However, if people are giving you contributions without expectation for a return, it is generally a gift to you.[81] Again, gift taxes are paid by the giver.

Before we leave this topic, we should mention that just because there is no tax deduction associated with gifts given on crowdfunding websites, it does not mean these cannot be worthwhile causes. There are certainly people who need help. As I have told many clients, if you do decide to give, just be careful and use your best judgment.

I want to give some investments to my kids. What should I give?

We talked earlier about the kiddie tax. Essentially, if your child has too much investment income, it will result in that income being taxed at your tax rate (a higher rate) than theirs (normally a lower tax rate). Therefore, if you want to give your child something from your investment portfolio, what can you do?

One option could be to give them investments that typically don't result in taxable income. For example, you might be able to give them stocks that historically have not paid a dividend or a fund that has a strategy not resulting in income. It should be noted that it is possible for a company or fund manager to break from historical precedent and pay a dividend. This is rare, though, because most fund managers and companies tend to follow what they have done in the past.

Another option may be to give your child municipal bonds or treasury bonds. Municipal bond interest is not taxable at the federal

81 This is a complicated area with several exceptions that can't possibly all be covered here. If you are thinking about receiving money through a crowdfunding website, you should talk to a tax practitioner about the details.

tax level (and in certain instances may not be taxable at the state level either). Treasury bonds are taxable at the federal level but may not be taxable at the state level. With all these options, the point is to consider giving a child an investment that won't generate too much taxable income.

Another option is using a loss harvesting approach with the investment portfolio of a child. As discussed above, loss harvesting involves selling offsetting gains and losses from the portfolio. The kiddie tax is only assessed on net investment income, so if you can offset some capital gains with capital losses, this could limit exposure to the kiddie tax as well.

It should be noted that not all of a child's investment income is subject to the kiddie tax. As we discussed, the first $2,700 of a child's investment income in 2025 is not subject to the parent's tax rate. So, another strategy could be simply trying to limit the amount of investment income rather than attempting to eliminate it.

Perhaps the most effective strategy of all may be the simplest—wait. Remember, the kiddie tax only applies while your child is . . . well, a kid! Once your child can no longer be claimed on your tax return as a dependent, the kiddie tax no longer applies. Investment income is taxed at your child's tax rate. Most of the time, when someone first enters the working world, their income is lower. Even if your child is no longer a dependent, there is a strong chance they are at a lower tax rate than you. If you wait until they are no longer a dependent and then transfer assets, this strategy may work well. As a reminder, you can transfer up to $19,000 to each child in 2025 and not pay any gift taxes on the transfer.

I have a different question . . .

Every year, around the middle of January, I see many television ads promoting do-it-yourself tax preparation. While these ads are often flashy, corny, and have even made me laugh a time or two, I think they miss the overall point for many people. Most people care less about the process of preparing their return. They want their tax return to be less of a black box. They want to know how they can influence the result—and maybe even learn how to save a few bucks!

Several years ago, I had a client who always seemed to be frustrated during tax season. She used to give a lot of clothes, household goods, and money to charity in the same amount each year, but the result on her return always seemed to be about the same. One day, I sat down with her and showed her how itemized and standard deductions worked. We came up with a very simple strategy. Instead of giving the same amount to charity each year, we would give twice as much one year and much less the next—one of the many strategies we've discussed in this book. In the years where she doubled up, she was able to itemize her deductions and take advantage of significantly larger refunds. In the years when she gave much less, she would just take the standard deduction and would end up with a small balance due. Overall, she was not giving anything more than what she had before. She was simply giving in a more tax-advantageous way.

For this client, it wasn't about how she was getting the return done, and there were no problems with the accuracy of the returns she was filing. It was about understanding where the numbers were coming from and how she could affect them. Once she took control of the return, she could directly affect the result. She could better predict what her refund or balance due would be and plan accordingly.

That is exactly what I hope you receive from this book as well. I hope this book has served (and will continue to serve) as a guide through Tax Land, unpacking the basics of the language, the landscape, and the most prominent factors that influence your tax return. While Tax Land may still not be somewhere you'd go for fun or on a vacation, I hope these tools make it less daunting to navigate each year—and that you're able to take greater control over your journey through it.

Obviously, there are only so many pages in this book. If you have a general question about taxes or want to know more about how you can directly influence your tax situation, feel free to reach out to me: david|petersprofessionaleducation.com. I will do my best to help or point you to a resource that might be useful. If you have something specific about your circumstances, feel free to reach out as well, and we can set up some time to have a conversation. I will do my best to help.

Thanks for reading . . . and happy filing season!

About the Author

David Peters is the founder and owner of Peters Professional Education (petersprofessionaleducation.com) and Peters Tax Preparation & Consulting, PC. He is also a financial advisor for Peters Financial, LLC. David has over twenty years of experience in financial services, including three years in the hedge fund industry and fourteen years in the insurance industry. David was the initial Chief Financial Officer at Compare.com—a position he held for over three years.

In addition to running his own professional education website, David is a National Instructor for the AICPA, Surgent, Kaplan, and Don Farmer Tax Seminars. He was a recipient of Surgent's Outstanding Discussion Leader award in 2019 and 2022, as well as the AICPA's Outstanding Facilitator Award in 2021 and 2023. He contributes regularly to various CPA publications, including NCACPA's Interim Report, SCACPA's CPA Report, and VSCPA's Disclosures. David was also a co-author of the 2018, 2019, and 2020 Virginia CPA Ethics courses—a required course for all CPAs licensed in the Commonwealth of Virginia.

www.ingramcontent.com/pod-product-compliance
Lightning Source LLC
Chambersburg PA
CBHW062014200326
41519CB00017B/4796
9781969935374